STUDY GUIDE

# NOTHING TO PROVE

---

## A STUDY IN THE GOSPEL OF JOHN

---

# JENNIE ALLEN

EIGHT SESSIONS

# CONTENTS

# ENGAGE WITH YOUR SMALL GROUP

An important part of personal growth is community. Together we will deal with the way we view God and how we are to spend our lives individually for Him. You may even need time outside of this small group to process with others your passions and gifts and purpose. Be intentional about pursuing deeper conversations with others throughout this process.

# COMMIT TO BEING CONSISTENT AND PRESENT

Commit to being present at your group meetings, barring an emergency, and arrange your schedule so you do not miss any part of this journey. Complete your lesson and Experiences before you come to the group meeting.

# STUDY DESIGN

For Group Study: In the first meeting, your group's study guides will be passed out and you will work through the Introduction lesson together. You will watch the video teaching as a group and have discussion based on the Conversation Cards as well.

For Independent Study: Each video teaching is included with your study guide. Simply follow the instructions on the inside cover for access to all the video sessions.

After the first week, each lesson in the study guide is meant to be completed on your own during the week before coming to the group meeting. These lessons may feel different from studies you have done in the past. They are very interactive. The beginning of each lesson will involve you, your Bible, and a pen, working through Scripture and listening to God's voice. Each lesson will conclude with four projects you can do to help you further process how to live God's Word.

Don't feel as if each lesson has to be finished in one sitting; take a few blocks of time throughout the week if you need to. The goal of this study is to dig deeply into Scripture and uncover how it applies to your life, to deeply engage the mind and the heart. Projects, stories, and Bible study all play a role in it. You may be drawing or journaling or interacting with the homeless.

# RESOURCES FOR FURTHER PERSONAL STUDY

www.biblegateway.com

# GROUND RULES FOR GROUP DISCUSSION

### BE CONCISE

Share your answers to the questions while protecting others' time for sharing. Be considerate. Don't be afraid to share with the group, but try not to dominate the conversation.

### KEEP GROUP MEMBERS' STORIES CONFIDENTIAL

Your group members will share sensitive and personal information with you, not with your husband or other friends. Protect each other by not allowing anything shared in the group to leave the group.

### RELY ON SCRIPTURE FOR TRUTH

Conventional, worldly wisdom has value, but it is not absolute truth. Only Scripture provides that. In your times of discussion, be careful not to equate good advice with God's Truth.

### NO COUNSELING

Work together to protect the group by not directing all attention on solving one person's problem. This is the place for confessing and discovery and applying truth together as a group. However, at times a member may need to dig even deeper with an outside counselor or talk with a friend outside of small group time. If that is you, don't be afraid to ask for help, or be sure and follow up with a member of the group.

# INTRODUCTION :: 1
## ARE YOU TIRED?

Last week, after years of tutors and tears and so much hard work and so little reward, my child received a diagnosis:

Dyslexia.

When I sat down to tell her, her eyes filled with tears. I was so worried this moment would define her view of herself for years to come.

And it will. But what I didn't expect is that the moment would set her free. After putting her head in my pillow and crying quietly for a few minutes, she looked up at me and said, "So there is a reason all this has been so hard for me?"

Her tears were relief!

The diagnosis helped explain the tension she's been feeling, why everything felt confusing no matter how hard she worked. It also meant the beginning of access to real help to meet her special needs.

Here's the thing: we begin this Bible study journey with words that may hurt initially. These diagnostic words are the opposite of everything Pinterest and Instagram are telling you. You may not like these words at first, but I think the truth in them will change everything.

## You are not enough.

We aren't. None of us. It's a universal diagnosis. But after we absorb the initial shock and hurt of that truth, it's usually followed by a wave of relief. We understand there is a reason we all feel a deep-in-our-bones problem. Then and only then can we allow Jesus to meet our enormous need.

I am so full of hope. Though we've been looking in all the wrong places for freedom, the door to true freedom is now found in a difficult diagnosis. It's a door to the most tender, kind, freeing, full hope.

A stark truth made my kid more free and full of hope than I've seen her in years. I'm believing the same for all of us.

## UNFORCED RHYTHMS

Are you tired? Worn out? Burned out on religion? Come to me. Get away with me and you'll recover your life. I'll show you how to take a real rest. Walk with me and work with me—watch how I do it. Learn the unforced rhythms of grace. I won't lay anything heavy or ill-fitting on you. Keep company with me and you'll learn to live freely and lightly.

**MATTHEW 11:28–30, MSG**

Are you tired?
Worn out?
Burned out on trying to measure up? Trying to prove yourself?

Maybe we are doing this life all wrong.

What if instead of waking up feeling empty, you awoke so full of wisdom and joy you couldn't help but give it away?

What if instead of living insecurely, you were watching God move through you in ways you couldn't believe?

What if instead of living in fear, you lived seeing potential?

What if instead of craving things you can't ever seem to get, you were fully satisfied and at peace?

What if instead of numbing out because you are tired of striving, you were at peace and could enjoy your life?

9

Jesus has a plan for our emptiness, our fatigue, our inadequacies, our sin.

> Let anyone who is thirsty come to me and drink. Whoever believes in me, as Scripture has said, rivers of living water will flow from within them.
>
> **JOHN 7:37–38**

Jesus is saying, *Keep coming back to Me and I will keep satisfying you. And out of that life with Me, you will overflow and bring life to others.*

## WHY ARE WE HERE?

We are here because it seems everything in us is fighting to keep us from getting to the water we are so thirsty for. We are here because we need each other in this fight and we need to remember there is water, and it is worth fighting the war currently blazing against us. I see it in every one of your eyes when we sit and talk about how you are really, actually doing. *War.* We hesitate to use the word because it sounds dramatic on a Tuesday, when the thought before this one was that tomorrow is trash day. But you feel it.

We want to think the war is out there, out there on the Internet, out there on the news, out there in other countries, out there in prisons, out there in everyone else.

So we say, "I'm okay." We think that and say that and try to mean it.

But the fight is always right here with us. So many of us stay thirsty, even though cold, living springs of water are right over the hill, completely available to us. Pretending to be at peace never ended a war. Engaging. Fighting. Coming together for great purposes. That is what ends wars.

*Nothing to Prove* is about taking hold of that which has already been given to us.

*Nothing to Prove* is about reminding ourselves from Scripture who we are in Christ.

Jesus is enough, so we don't have to be. In fact, it is downright arrogant to keep trying to be. The reality is that He is the enough we could never be.

## I don't have to prove anything because Jesus proved everything.

But we barely know what that means, much less how to rest in that truth. Instead we strive, we perform, we work harder, or we numb out. Why? There is an enemy deceiving us, telling us to go anywhere except the water. Not only are we never satisfied, we also end up depleting every gift and person God has given us here to enjoy.

## IF I WERE YOUR ENEMY...

*If I were your enemy, this is what I would do:*

*Make you believe you need permission to lead.*
*Make you believe you are helpless.*
*Make you believe you are insignificant.*
*Make you believe that God wants your decorum and behavior.*
*And for years these lies have been sufficient to shut down much of the church.*
*But now, many of you are awake. You are in the Word and on your knees. God is moving through you, and you are getting dangerous. You are starting to get free and lead other people to freedom. The old lies no longer bind you.*

*So if I were your enemy, **I would make you numb and distract you from God's story.***
*Technology, social media, Netflix, travel, food, comfort. I would not tempt you with notably bad things, or you would get suspicious. I would*

*distract you with everyday comforts that slowly feed you a different story and make you forget God.*

*Then you would dismiss the Spirit leading you, loving you, and comforting you. Then you would start to love comfort more than surrender and obedience and souls.*
*If that didn't work, I would attack your identity. I would make you believe you had to prove yourself.*
*Then you would focus on yourself instead of God.*

*Friends would become enemies.*
*Teammates would become competition.*
*You would isolate yourself and think you are not enough.*
*You would get depressed and be ungrateful for your story.*
*Or,*
*You would compare and believe you are better than others.*
*You would judge people who need God.*
*You would condemn them rather than love and invite them in.*
*You would gossip and destroy and tear down other works of God.*

*Either way you would lose your joy, because your eyes would be fixed on yourself and people instead of on Jesus.*

*And if that didn't work,* ***I would intoxicate you with the mission of God rather than God Himself.***
*Then you would worship a cause instead of Jesus.*
*You would fight each other to have the most important roles.*
*You would burn out from striving.*
*You would think that success is measured by the results you see.*
*You would build platforms for applause rather than to display God.*

*Then all of your time and effort would be spent on becoming important rather than on knowing Jesus and loving people. The goals would be to gather followers, earn fancy job titles, publish books, build big ministries rather than to seek the souls of men and the glory of God.*

*And if that didn't work, **I would make you suffer.***
*Then maybe you would think God is evil rather than good.*
*Your faith would shrink.*
*You would get bitter and weary and tired rather than flourish and grow and become more like Christ.*
*You would try to control your life rather than step into the plans He has for you.*

The enemy is telling you that freedom is only found in finally proving to yourself and to the world that …
you are important;
you are in control;
you are liked;                       Good
you are happy;
you are enough.

We must remember: "The thief comes only to steal and kill and destroy" (John 10:10). So we have the most epic eternal battle on our hands every moment of every day. But Jesus says, *I have come to give you life and to give you life to the fullest.*

This is a fight for your hope and joy and peace and satisfaction. Strike that. This is full-on war to steal the core of who you are and who you were meant to be. It is a fight for your life. It is a fight for our lives.

Hear the promise of God:

> Forget the former things; do not dwell on the past. See, I am doing a new thing! Now it springs up; do you not perceive it? I am making a way in the wilderness and streams in the wasteland.
>
> **ISAIAH 43:18–19**

## Jesus.

He is the way in the desert. He is the new spring, containing all we crave and long for. We are going to look at Jesus' life throughout the Book of John: the way He lived, what He valued, where He went, why He went, what He hoped for, what He wanted. And then we are going to dream a little, step out of the accidental boxes we have erected around us, and live like Him.

## Revolutionary concept: live like Jesus.

Fully engaged with our whole hearts, minds, bodies, and emotions. Fully connected to the people around us. Fully present through the pain and the joy. Fully aware of the need around us and the part we could play in meeting it. Jesus is not only our means of salvation, He is also the example of how we should live.

Jesus lived overflowing God and it was the most compelling life ever lived. And then, He shockingly called us to live life just like Him. But like a lot of other humans we settle for a lesser life.

> My people have committed two sins: They have forsaken me,
> the spring of living water, and have dug their own cisterns,
> broken cisterns that cannot hold water.
>
> **JEREMIAH 2:13**

Christian, inside of you flow streams of living water. Why would we ever go back to storing water in broken man-made places?

So before we begin, we have to soberly assess where we are.

Maybe you're like me, so hard on yourself. My broken cistern is that I try to be enough in myself, leaving me exhausted. Or perhaps you are someone who thinks, *I will go out and get enough. I will fill up broken cisterns and make a way for myself.* But again we end up depleted and empty and tired. Why? Because this world does not have what we are craving.

Or perhaps you are just over it altogether and have numbed out because it feels impossible to even hope that there could be satisfaction.

Consider: The problem with being numb is that it is less detectable than sadness or anger or joy. People don't often even think about it, except that usually just under the surface, there is a nagging sense that something isn't right.

*As we begin this journey together, take 10 minutes to answer the following questions.*

What consumes most of your thoughts? Why?

BROTHER + SISTER - DISTANT

NO FAMILY

What consumes most of your time? Why?

What are you most often afraid of? Why?

Are you striving? In what ways?

Are you numbing? Why?

How are you and Jesus right now?

What do you hope for in this study?

# A VISION FOR NOTHING TO PROVE

A person who holds even a smidgen of faith can be a powerful, radical, dangerous force in the kingdom of God, seeing the impossible take place (Matt. 17:20).

A sincere faith in Jesus and all He wants to do around us wakes us up, rattles our lives, shifts every perspective, issues hope in pain, and ignites mission.

I am praying that this Bible study would make our God so big that any moment we miss of Him and the life He has for us is the greatest loss to us.

Jesus, move a generation to draw near to You and believe You at Your word.

# SEE ::

Watch video session 1 now.

Use streaming code on inside cover or DVD.

# FULFILLED :: 2
## THE END OF THIRST

When I looked up *joy* in the thesaurus I found a list of fantastic words, the sum of which are actually better descriptions of what I want us to discuss here.

*bliss*
*cheer*
*delight*
*wonder*
*elation*
*glee*
*satisfaction*

Several years ago, my husband, Zac, and I prayed, "God, we'll do anything you want us to do," and since then our lives have radically changed. Just about every part of our lives is different. And I would never go back. Our son Cooper, born in Rwanda, is in our family because of that prayer. I am writing these words along with many before them because of that prayer. My husband is in Ethiopia today helping build businesses and jobs because of that prayer. IF:Gathering exists because of that prayer. I would never go back. However, over these years an urgency to please and obey God has strangled much of the wonder, delight, elation, satisfaction, and just plain fun out of my life.

Like a pendulum, I swung from life is about my happiness to life is about difficult things.

And so as we approach this week, the question before us is …

## Does God want us to be fulfilled and happy here?

It's my fear that we have somehow subtly picked up the belief that it is wrong to be happy. Maybe it's caused by the suffering of friends nearby or the suffering all over the world. Or perhaps we're influenced by the crushing pressures of work and life. Maybe it's because fun has become more of an escape than an attribute of people who know God. Or could it be that following Jesus has become duty rather than delight?

Jesus lived with purpose and joy, delighting to do His Father's will. He called others to follow Him in this kind of life. He was clear about where the fulfillment they looked for would be found.

Satisfaction comes when we lay down this life and live for the next.

Jesus had His mind full of hope for the next life; He came from heaven and knew it well. However, even with heaven in clear sight, Jesus lived fully in this life. He created experiences for the people around Him to see more of God—turning water to wine as they celebrated a wedding, eating unforgettable long meals with strangers and friends, celebrating the extravagance of perfume being poured out for Him. Jesus created moments that those He loved could never forget. And He chose to enjoy the people around Him and the work He had here.

Are we living the same way?

# STUDY ::

Read JOHN 2:1–12

# CULTURAL CONTEXT

In Jesus' day, weddings were a community affair that lasted many days. They were hosted by the bridegroom and his family. It's likely Mary was related in some way to the groom's family, which is why she felt so responsible for this mistake. Running out of wine would have been a tremendous embarrassment to the family.

# RESPOND

What do you notice about Jesus' actions and words in this passage?

What do you learn about Jesus' priorities?

Describe the details you observe about:

The setting:

Mary:

Jesus:

The other people present:

The bridegroom:

The jars Jesus had the men fill:

The wine:

How did those who knew Jesus performed the miracle respond?

Why do you think Jesus did this as His first public miracle?

The world operates completely differently than Jesus. He was bringing an entirely unfamiliar, wholly other system into place, and He launched His new way right out of the gate with a symbol. Water to wine. But not just any water to wine. He chose to turn the water found in the ceremonial religious cleansing jars to wine for a wedding. And not just typical cheap table wine but the very best wine.

Is it possible that the reason we are so unfulfilled, even those of us who say we follow Jesus, is that we are still going to religious jars or drinking cheap wine, when the new way and the new wine is fully available?

## RELIGIOUS JARS VS. JESUS

The nature of religion is that it insists upon a moral requirement. You measure up and you are accepted. The jars at the wedding were a part of the religious system at the time. The stone jars Jesus asked the servants to fill with water represented the Jewish purification traditions, not those prescribed in the Old Testament, but the man-made rules the religious leaders had added to the law. Do you think it was coincidence that these were the jars Jesus asked the men to fill? He leaned in specifically to a symbol of their striving and working to earn God's favor.

We have these same tendencies—often inadvertently striving and trying to win God's favor. Without even realizing it, we begin to perform for God, rather than enjoy God. We subtly begin to fear disappointing God, rather than rest in His steadfast love.

Religion and living in the rhythms of this world have taught us that we must measure up. We must hit the mark. We must be awesome. This leads to feelings of failure and regret and fear seeping into our relationship with Jesus and taking captive our thoughts and emotions. We let this happen because we are still going to jars of religion rather than the flowing delight and fulfillment of Jesus' new way.

Wine in the Bible is often used as a metaphor. In fact, it's used as one of the most significant metaphors for the most important event in history. Near the end of Jesus' life, at the final supper with His disciples, He poured wine and said of it, *This cup that is poured out for you is the new covenant in My blood. When you drink of it, remember Me. Every time you drink or eat, remember that My body was broken for you and My blood was spilled for you, all to fulfill a promise, to confirm a new covenant between God and you* (Luke 22:17–20).

So what is the new covenant?

The wine would be a symbol of the greatest news on earth.

"This is the covenant I will make with the people of Israel
after that time," declares the LORD.
"I will put my law in their minds
and write it on their hearts.
I will be their God,
and they will be my people.
No longer will they teach their neighbor,
or say to one another, 'Know the LORD,'
because they will all know me,
from the least of them to the greatest,"
declares the LORD.
"For I will forgive their wickedness
and will remember their sins no more."

**JEREMIAH 31:33–34**

In speaking of a new covenant, he makes the first one
obsolete. And what is becoming obsolete and growing old is
ready to vanish away.

**HEBREWS 8:13, ESV**

The death of Christ, remembered with wine, promises the opportunity to be near to our God, to be in relationship with Him, to know Him, and to receive His grace.

Forever the new wine would mean:
the end of our sin;
the end of measuring up;
the end of proving ourselves;
the beginning of what we were made for—nearness to God.

## CHEAP WINE VS. JESUS

Until we regularly enjoy the rhythms of grace Jesus is promising, we tend to wear out from striving. We move from our own futile effort to becoming numb.

We were built to crave pleasure, joy, happiness. God built us for it, and when we don't find it in Him and come to the end of ourselves, we look for something to numb our reality.

As a culture, our God-given craving for fulfillment has driven us past God Himself, who was meant to be the fulfillment of our desires, toward a drug that helps us cope with our discontentment and inadequacies: entertainment. As a generation, we are addicted to it. We have a constant need to occupy our minds and time with diversions and amusements. For some, that may be alcohol and for others exercise. For some, it may be sports for their kids or vacations or gossip. It could mean chasing a job that is more challenging or a marriage that seems more exciting. Some even seek that diversion in meaningful work or charity, even religious activity. Some seek it by refreshing Facebook and some through the rush of pornography.

Joy: the emotion of great delight or happiness caused by something exceptionally good or satisfying; keen pleasure; elation.[1]

Entertainment: an agreeable occupation for the mind; diversion; amusement.[2]

But just like the metaphorical cheap wine, these pursuits never satisfy us. These are the drugs of the day, and, friends, we are all wasting our lives on them. But what is the exchange? If we lay down the drug of our day which diverts us from God and actual wonder, delight, and joy, what are we to pick up? Look ahead at a moment when Jesus is speaking of this war for us—the war for our minds, our salvation, our well-being. Jesus describes Himself as the shepherd and us as His sheep.

> Truly, truly, I say to you, I am the door of the sheep. I am the door. If anyone enters by me, he will be saved and will go in and out and find pasture. The thief comes only to steal and kill and destroy. I came that they may have life and have it abundantly. I am the good shepherd. The good shepherd lays down his life for the sheep.
>
> **JOHN 10:7,9–11, ESV**

In these verses, what is Jesus after?

What is the thief after?

What is the only door to the abundant life we were built for?

How do these verses affect your view of Jesus' desires for your life now?

Scripture is clear we are saved once and for all by grace and through faith in our great Shepherd, Jesus Christ (Eph. 2:4–9), and our eternal place as children of God is secured by the loving, gracious hand of our God (John 10:27–30).

But I believe that until we get to heaven, every day we decide if we will walk through the door that provides the very best wine—the most abundant, freeing, fully focused, un-numb, joy-filled life. Or, do we listen to the unrelenting voice of the enemy and choose the addictive and unfulfilling cheap wine?

Have you ever tasted Jesus' abundant fulfillment here?

Write some examples of times you have experienced Jesus fulfilling you.

WHO ARE YOU, LORD? & WHAT DO YOU WANT FOR ME?

Read Ephesians 2:4–10. In light of what you read, answer the questions above.

# DIGGING DEEPER *(OPTIONAL)*

Some of you may want to pursue deeper
Bible study. This section is for you.

Jesus intentionally chose to make wine for His first miracle. Throughout
Scripture, wine is used as a symbol of joy.

*Look up the following verses and make notes on how wine
represents joy:*

Genesis 27:27–28


Deuteronomy 7:13; 33:28


Psalm 104:14–15


Ecclesiastes 9:7; 10:19


Jeremiah 31:12

The people at the wedding would have known these Scriptures. How do you think this affected their understanding of Jesus' miracle?

We also see Jesus talk about wine in Matthew 26:29. When does Jesus say He will drink wine again? What will that day be like (Rev. 19:6–9)?

# EXPERIENCES

I find it interesting that when Jesus was laying the law down He didn't leave it at "love the Lord your God." He was clear that we are to love Him with all our hearts and with all our souls and with all our minds (Matt. 22:37). He was specific. But often in our study of God's Word we let loving God with our minds be enough.

In the next few pages you will find a variety of experiences. These experiences are an effort to take what you learn with your mind and move it into your heart and soul and into your everyday life. Some of these things may seem silly to you or make you feel uncomfortable. I suggest reading through all of them on the first day to gather any supplies needed and to make plans to do all of the experiences at some point during the week. Hopefully these experiences will push you out of numbness and nearer to Jesus.

# BE

In his great work entitled *The Mortification of Sin*, John Owen says, "Be killing sin, or it will be killing you."[3] I believe a prominent way the enemy numbs us and addicts us to entertainment rather than joy is with technology.

*Choose a day this week to take 24 hours and fast from electronics such as your TV, phone, iPad, computer, and so forth. Hide your devices. Don't touch them for 24 hours. It is nearly impossible to completely do this. But unless you do it completely, you will probably get sucked back in.*

## SUGGESTIONS:

- If you have children, instruct the school or childcare to call your spouse or relative if something happens.

- If you have work commitments that require use of technology, you may need to do this activity on a weekend. Plan accordingly.

- Set up an email responder that you are out for the day and will return emails the next day.

- Do not announce your "fast" on social media or to anyone. Scripture is clear about this (Matt. 6:16).

*At the conclusion of the 24 hours, write what you observed about yourself, God, and technology below.*

# CREATE

Jesus is a masterful experience-creator. He is never boring, never what everyone is expecting.

Create an experience for some of your friends or family just for the fun of it!

The only guidelines are:
It has to be fun.
It has to be inexpensive.
It has to contain something you all have never done or tried before.
It has to be memorable.

Some of you are naturally creative and you love this! Others of you may need to brainstorm with someone—that is okay. Seek out help if you can't think of something. I promise you will not regret the time you take to enjoy life a little more and make some new memories.

What are you going to do?

When are you going to do it?

# MEDITATE

*Spend some time alone with Jesus. Here is a passage to read and pray through.*

> O God, you are my God; earnestly I seek you; my soul thirsts for you; my flesh faints for you, as in a dry and weary land where there is no water. So I have looked upon you in the sanctuary, beholding your power and glory. Because your steadfast love is better than life, my lips will praise you. So I will bless you as long as I live; in your name I will lift up my hands. My soul will be satisfied as with fat and rich food, and my mouth will praise you with joyful lips, when I remember you upon my bed, and meditate on you in the watches of the night; for you have been my help, and in the shadow of your wings I will sing for joy. My soul clings to you; your right hand upholds me. But those who seek to destroy my life shall go down into the depths of the earth; they shall be given over to the power of the sword; they shall be a portion for jackals. But the king shall rejoice in God; all who swear by him shall exult, for the mouths of liars will be stopped.
>
> **PSALM 63, ESV**

What does it mean to earnestly seek God? Is that the status of your heart right now?

Are you currently in a dry and weary land? Explain.

How is it possible to have joy even in the midst of such a time?

# RISK

*Sit down with someone close to you, a good friend or family member, and ask them these questions. Be brave. I know this will make you feel vulnerable, but better to risk a conversation like this than to be stuck for years.*

Do I seem joyful to you?

If not, why do you think I'm not?

Do you see any patterns in my life that may be stealing my joy?

When have you seen me most fulfilled?

What is one thing I could change in the next month that would cause me to live more content?

Exhort one another every day, as long as it is called "today," that none of you may be hardened by the deceitfulness of sin.

**HEBREWS 3:13, ESV**

# CONCLUSION

Friends, what if abundant joy, bliss, wonder, and pleasure were ours, but we just kept missing those things because we're either trying to work our way to God or numbing ourselves with fleeting entertainment?

I am learning to pick up books that show me more of Jesus instead of turning on Netflix. I am learning to call friends over for chili instead of surfing Facebook. I am learning to look my kids in the eyes instead of stare at my phone. Our family is choosing to eat outside and laugh and have game nights and I am learning that the rhythms of gracious living are sacred and pleasing to Jesus. I want to enjoy God's gifts but never give them too much power in my life. I want to see that Jesus is better, better than any cheap substitute I may crave.

I am getting there and I pray the same for you.

# SEE ::

Watch video session 2 now.

Use streaming code on inside cover or DVD.

# CONNECTED :: 3
## THE END OF LONELINESS

*The New York Times* once posted an article entitled "To Fall in Love with Anyone, Do This."[4] Like everyone else who read the title, I had to know what "this" was that could cause any two random people to fall in love. The article was based on a study conducted by Dr. Arthur Aron, who successfully caused two complete strangers to fall in love.

The two strangers sat across from one another and asked a series of 36 questions that gradually increased in intimacy, moving from questions like #2, "Would you like to be famous?" to #30, "When did you last cry in front of another person?"

At the end of the 36 questions, the two strangers were to stare into each other's eyes for four minutes.

Have you ever tried to stare into someone's eyes for four whole minutes?

It is no small thing to stare into someone's soul for four minutes and all the while allow them to stare into yours. I think the risk usually proves too much. Most people look away. Connection is like that. Most people move away from it when it comes too close.

## Connection costs our whole selves.
## Connection risks all that we are.

And yet we still all crave connection more than just about anything else on earth.

I venture to say most of us feel a constant twinge of loneliness. Even though we are surrounded by people, we can still miss each other. We can be sitting in the same room or driving in a car together and miss opportunities to really see each other, to really hear each other. And we move on just like this, missing Jesus, too.

## How badly do you want to live more connected?

Jesus was so present in His life here. He chose to have intentional conversations with those around Him, but also chose to steal away and pursue time with His Father. He was God the Son, and yet there was no greater priority than time with His Father. Jesus' intimate relationship with the Father and obedience to Him defined and directed everything Jesus did while on earth. He clearly says in John 4, "My food is to do the will of him who sent me and to finish his work" (v. 34).

Let's see what it might look like for us to live with the same devotion.

# STUDY ::

Read JOHN 4:1–43

## CULTURAL CONTEXT

Samaritans and Jews hated each other. This hatred went back hundreds of years to the fall of the Northern Kingdom to Assyria. After the nation fell, Assyrians deported most of the Jews, then brought in Gentiles to resettle the land. Intermarriage between the remaining Jews and the pagan Gentiles took place along with worship of foreign idols. Full-blooded Jews looked on the Samaritans as unclean half-breeds. By Jesus' time, the relationship between Jews and Samaritans was so strained that most Jews avoided traveling through Samaria at all costs.

## RESPOND

Describe the woman at the well.

Most women in those days got water in the cool of the morning or evening. Why was this woman there during the heat of the day?

55

Describe Jesus' interaction with her.

How did Jesus begin the conversation? Why is this important?

What barriers did they press through to carry on this conversation?

What were some of the results of this intentional conversation?

Describe the water Jesus was offering.

Describe the food Jesus chose to feast on.

What convicts you most from this passage?

## ACCEPTED AND CONNECTED

It is the most secure place in the world to be connected to Jesus. The source of what we know about healthy relationships is found in our connection with Jesus and His unconditional love for us. The health of our relationships with others flows out of the reality that we are completely accepted and loved by Jesus.

Finding our worth in Christ takes the pressure off our relationships with those we love. We can live without having to prove ourselves to them or have them meet all of our needs.

Sitting in the deepest part of us is an enormous desire to connect. We crave intimate connection with our people more than nearly any other thing.

Isn't it just beautiful how much of this chapter in John is devoted to a conversation with an adulterous woman? Jesus was so fully present with her and fully aware of her needs and committed to meeting her needs, needs she didn't even realize she had. I think of how often I avoid intentional conversations. It seems too much trouble to engage deeply with neighbors or sometimes even with my kids. It is easier to brush by people and in turn brush by our lives.

We are rarely fully present with God and others. Jesus had complete knowledge of His eternal home and yet while His feet were on this earth, He chose to live fully present in the dirt with His people. Living intentionally present takes discipline. It means a full-on war against an entire culture that prizes busyness. Even our churches can keep us too busy.

At some point in her time with Jesus, this woman went from wandering and searching and hiding to free and engaged and purposeful. She had probably been going to the well alone for years, hoping to hide from the whispers and judgment. But after being with Jesus, she boldly ran back to the town and shared the very thing she had been trying to hide from them and she was even joyful about it! She testified about the Savior who changed her life in mere minutes.

## SHE WENT FROM:

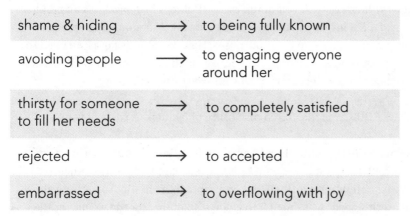

| | | |
|---|---|---|
| shame & hiding | ⟶ | to being fully known |
| avoiding people | ⟶ | to engaging everyone around her |
| thirsty for someone to fill her needs | ⟶ | to completely satisfied |
| rejected | ⟶ | to accepted |
| embarrassed | ⟶ | to overflowing with joy |

For the last year or more I have met with three of my dearest friends for lunch every week. In our conversations we go to the hardest places, the places you usually keep tucked in the very back of your secret closet. We bring out the very darkest parts of our lives and stories, and lay them out. Then together we start to discover what God wants for us.

A few weeks ago my people confronted me, because that's what we do. It's so lovely. And painful.

Each of them said I was playing it safe, holding back. And as I write this today I am still processing their words. If you have read very much of my

59

writing or heard me speak, you know I lay it all out: my mistakes, my fears, my sin. I don't hide my imperfections and quickly seem to sabotage most pedestals I'm placed on.

But I am learning there is a difference between vulnerability and transparency. This is how I see it.

I will be vulnerable with you in this study. But let's be honest, it's an edited version of all of my worst thoughts and moments. Vulnerability is precious and useful and can serve great purposes. However, it is as far as we need to go with most acquaintances and for sure as far as we should go on Facebook. But transparency is necessary with your closest people.

VULNERABILITY is the edited disclosure of feelings or parts of your life.

TRANSPARENCY is exposing the unedited, unfiltered, unflattering parts of your soul. I think it is very difficult to even want to be fully connected when we are fighting subtle shame or disappointment. But something about encountering Jesus was enough to change all of that for the woman at the well. The foundation of her identity shifted.

## Encounter Jesus.

It sounds wonderful, but we have to make space and time to be with Him. This week, the Experiences are going to lead you into intentional time with Jesus. I cannot imagine a more life-changing pursuit than intentional time with the Savior.

WHO ARE YOU, LORD?  &  WHAT DO YOU WANT FOR ME?

*Read James 5:13–16,19–20. In light of what you read, answer the questions above.*

# DIGGING DEEPER (OPTIONAL)

While studying the story of the Samaritan woman, we noted some differences between the Jews and Samaritans. We also need to consider differences between our culture and theirs.

Read John 8:1–11.

What could have happened to this woman if Jesus had not been present?

Read Leviticus 20:10 and Deuteronomy 22:22.

What does the Old Testament law (accepted by Jews and Samaritans) say the punishment for adultery is?

What was Jesus' response in John 8?

Read Mark 10:2–12.

By the time of Jesus, the Pharisees had twisted the law to mean a man could divorce his wife for any reason that displeased him, such as her inability to have children or for simply burning his dinner.

Reread Jesus' words to the Pharisees in Mark 10. Jesus says Moses allowed divorce because of their "hardness of heart" (v. 5, ESV). If any of the Samaritan woman's marriages ended in divorce, what could have been the reasons?

Look at the Samaritan woman's story again in John 4. While she was currently living with a man she wasn't married to, what do you think the rest of her story might have been before she met Jesus?

How does this change your understanding of Jesus' interaction with her?

# CONNECT
## ... WITH GOD

Read Hebrews 13:5; Romans 12:2.

What distracts me from my time with God?
*Example: My long to-do list.*

How can I practically remove these distractions based on the Scriptures? *Example: Turn off my phone.*

## ... WITH PEOPLE

Read Ecclesiastes 5:18–20; Ephesians 5:15–16; Colossians 4:3–6.

What keeps me from being present in my relationships? *Example: Fear of judgment.*

How can I be more present in my relationships based on the Scriptures? *Example: Be a better listener (James 1:19).*

# GATHER

Buy or build a fire pit in your backyard. I believe deeply in fire pits and food and Adirondack chairs. You can find affordable ones online or at a local hardware store. String some lights and invite your family or closest friends over for dessert.

Roast marshmallows, turn off your phones, and answer some questions together around the fire.

Go first and talk about struggles you are facing, sins God is freeing you from. Also share what God is teaching you as you walk through these times.

Then, ask these questions:

What are you struggling with right now? How can we help?

What do we need to know about you to really know you?

What things are you tempted to hold back from the people closest to you?

Why do you hold back?

# BE

Perhaps if you already meet regularly with Jesus, this will be easy for you. But if you do not, I thought it would be helpful to try this experiment for five days. See if this sacred protected time and space feels like something you want to keep in your life.

- Identify a place in your home to be your quiet place. It could be your favorite chair, a porch, or maybe a closet.

- Put a basket in your quiet place that contains your Bible, a few books, a candle, journal, and pen.

This week set your alarm 30 minutes earlier than normal. And at least five times this week, spend your extra 30 minutes praying, journaling, and reading your Bible. Meet with Jesus.

As you get to the end of the five days, write about the experience here.

What did this time mean to you?

How did this time affect your day?

What barriers are keeping you from making this part of your routine every week?

# MEDITATE

*Find a quiet place and time, perhaps the space you designated in the previous experience. Read and meditate on this passage.*

Underline the words Psalm 84 uses to describe the person who is in the presence of God.

How lovely is your dwelling place, O LORD of hosts! My soul longs, yes, faints for the courts of the LORD; my heart and flesh sing for joy to the living God. Even the sparrow finds a home, and the swallow a nest for herself, where she may lay her young, at your altars, O LORD of hosts, my King and my God. Blessed are those who dwell in your house, ever singing your praise! Blessed are those whose strength is in you, in whose heart are the highways to Zion. As they go through the Valley of Baca they make it a place of springs; the early rain also covers it with pools. They go from strength to strength; each one appears before God in Zion. O LORD God of hosts, hear my prayer; give ear, O God of Jacob! Behold our shield, O God; look on the face of your anointed! For a day in your courts is better than a thousand elsewhere. I would rather be a doorkeeper in the house of my God than dwell in the tents of wickedness. For the LORD God is a sun and shield; the LORD bestows favor and honor. No good thing does he withhold from those who walk uprightly. O LORD of hosts, blessed is the one who trusts in you!

**PSALM 84, ESV**

# CONCLUSION

My daughter Kate and I went on a date recently and I pulled out the conversation cards provided for you this week. I asked her, "What have you been dreaming about lately?" She laughed telling me about how fun science is to her right now.

She has been studying the brain, which has prompted her to do a lot of extra reading on neuroscience. She thinks she may want to go into the field as a career someday. She thinks she could help kids with autism.

I sat slack-jawed, in awe, of my beautiful, intelligent, compassionate daughter who has the habit of growing up right in front of my eyes. I kept thinking, *I could have missed this moment if I hadn't asked this question.*

Then she picked up a card and read it to me, "Mom, what do you most fear?"

I knew my answer immediately, "I most fear that one day you will resent my work. I fear that you would resent it because it often pulled me away from time with you." Kate's face lit up as she shared the antidote to my greatest problem.

"Mom, I could never resent your work. I love that you help people and I hope one day I can help people, too. Don't be afraid of that anymore."

Oh, thank You, God, for meeting us in our most tender places. Thank You for pressing into our fears and our mistakes for our healing.

The risk is worth it. Be known and know. Ask the brave questions and give the risky answers.

# SEE ::

Watch video session 3 now.

Use streaming code on inside cover or DVD.

# REST ::
## THE END OF STRIVING

4

All through grade school I took ballet from Ms. Karen. I wore the same outfit every week—pink tights, a pink leotard, and little pink ballet shoes with a tiny string of a bow. Practice was regular and ordinary. No lights, no crowds, no glitter, no makeup. It couldn't have been more plain.

But once a year we would put on outfits with glitter and go to one of the biggest stages in our town. In those moments, it would occur to me, *I could be an epic dancer. I could be a star.* So in an effort to stand out from all of the other eight-year-old girls in the exact same costume, with the exact same dirty little ballet shoes, I would strive. I mean, I couldn't really strive in my actual dance. It was simple and choreographed, and I wasn't going to bust out all rogue little dancer girl. But in my soul I would strive—strive to be seen, strive to smile the biggest, strive to be noticed somehow.

Isn't it funny I remember that feeling? And how silly. I was one of thirty eight-year-olds in the same outfit.

## Are you tired? Weary? What's the cause?

Is it really the work you have been given to do or is it the striving in your soul that makes you tired? This week we are studying John 6, where Jesus feeds the five thousand with a few fish and loaves, and He walks on water in the midst of a storm. These beautiful moments display the power of God over all circumstances and the power of God to take our small offerings and turn them into eternal work.

Knowing God and tasting heaven should cause us to rest rather than strive. Rest is a discipline and an act of obedience. We think of rest as crawling into bed and binge-watching a season of our favorite show. But true rest is something that fills our souls and empowers us to create and intentionally live life. Rest is believing God can do anything, then stepping back and letting Him.

## Is your soul tired?

# STUDY ::

Read JOHN 6

# CULTURAL CONTEXT

When Jesus challenged Philip about where they would purchase bread to feed the large crowd, Philip responded that even if they had two hundred denarii, it would not purchase enough food. A denarii was a day's wage in the time of Jesus. So, not counting non-working days and feast days, two hundred denarii would have equaled several months' wages.

# RESPOND *(JOHN 6:1–15)*

Describe the problem.

Compare and contrast Philip's and Andrew's responses to the problem.

Describe Jesus' posture and actions in this passage.

What were the results of the miracle?

# RESPOND *(JOHN 6:16 – 21)*

Describe the setting.

Describe the disciples.

Describe Jesus.

In these two miracles what do you think Jesus was communicating to His disciples?

# RESPOND *(JOHN 6:22–71)*

What were the crowds wanting from Jesus?

Describe the "work" that God wants from men (vv. 27–28).

Write down all that Jesus offered them (vv. 35–70).

Did the masses want what Jesus was offering? Why not?

Who did want what He was offering? Why?

## TRUST = REST

Every section of this chapter reveals aspects of what it means to rest, what it means to trust. Isn't that the same thing?

When Jesus promises us rest, He is almost always talking about soul rest. It's why all the ways we try to rest our souls don't actually make us feel very rested—TV, sleep, Facebook surfing, and so forth. They all fall short because nothing but Jesus can issue rest for our chaotic insides.

In fact, most of the ways we try to rest actually make our insides more chaotic. Surfing Facebook can end with us angry over someone's post or comparing our lives to our friends'. Binge-watching a show can suck us into fictional stress and distract us from connecting with our real-life people. Even taking a vacation can become chaotic with plans and preparation and possibly disappointed expectations.

> Lifting up his eyes, then, and seeing that a large crowd was coming toward him, Jesus said to Philip, "Where are we to buy bread, so that these people may eat?" He said this to test him, for he himself knew what he would do. Philip answered him, "Two hundred denarii worth of bread would not be enough for each of them to get a little."
>
> **JOHN 6:5–7, ESV**

In these verses we see Jesus state the impossible task before Philip, testing him. It seems Jesus went out of His way to show Philip and the rest of the disciples it could not be done in their power.

Then with shocking ease and out of a place of relationship and trust with His Father, Jesus modeled for them and us the freedom from striving and the joy of dependence.

Jesus fully trusted in the exceeding abundance of His Father, God.

Do we?

Last night I sat up late processing all of this with Zac. We remembered how many times we have all but lost our minds with fear about the future, fear about provision, fear about pleasing people, fear about sickness, fear about measuring up.

## FEAR = STRIVING

Philip believed there wasn't enough. Philip believed they were in this with only their own resources. But Andrew had at least enough faith to bring Jesus whatever they had, even though it was insufficient.

And then, almost to drive home the point even further, in the chaos of a storm, Jesus walks on water to His men. He could have gotten on the boat before it left the shore, but then they would have missed His overwhelming power over all of the chaos. We may feel crushed by the fear of real circumstances, but Jesus is above the circumstances. He moves through chaos as if it doesn't exist, because in light of eternity and His unending resources and power, our chaos here is a small storm that Jesus walks right through with us.

Jesus is the living, unending water and the Bread of life when all other breads run out. He keeps giving in abundance. Our soul rest is not based on the absence of trouble and chaos. Our soul rest is based on the never-failing character of our good, capable, rich Father God.

Take a minute and lay out your fears.

What are you afraid of?

What are you worried about?

If God wants to rescue us from chaos, He can. But what if He doesn't? What if He allows the storm so that we might know His power to walk right through it with us? Perhaps the chaos continues so that He might conform us to the image of His Son.

In the middle of the storm we need to remember some important things. This world is not our home. This life is not the end. There is nothing man can do to us, nothing sacred that can be taken from us. We are as secure as Jesus was on that water because we know our Father God is with us. He has prepared a forever place for us. And one day all things will be made right.

Actually, through studying with you the last few weeks I realized my hopes weren't big enough for this God. He doesn't just give us what we need now; He gives us what we need forever, with no fear of it ever running out.

Joy

Peace

Hope

Love

Presence

Rest in spades—forever.

WHO ARE YOU, LORD?     &     WHAT DO YOU WANT FOR ME?

Read Isaiah 30:15–22. In light of what you read, answer the questions above.

# DIGGING DEEPER *(OPTIONAL)*

In John 6:25–70, Jesus interacts with the crowd concerning His true purpose. Read the following passages and note the crowd's questions and complaints, followed by Jesus' response.

Read John 6:25–27.

The crowd's question:

Jesus' response:

Read John 6:28–29.

The crowd's question:

Jesus' response:

Read John 6:30–40.

The crowd's questions:

Jesus' responses:

Read John 6:41–51.

The crowd's complaint:

Jesus' response:

Read John 6:52–59.

The crowd's confusion:

Jesus' response:

Read John 6:60–69.

## The disciples' complaint:
(Note: The use of "disciples" in this passage denotes a larger number of people who were following Jesus. John distinguishes between this group and the twelve apostles by using the term "the Twelve.")

Jesus' response:

Simon Peter's response:

How did the people miss Jesus' true purpose?

How do people miss it today?

Is your response to Jesus more like the disciples' in verse 60, or Simon Peter's response in verse 68? Explain.

# REFLECT

Write the thoughts, feelings, and actions that define the times when you are:

| TRUSTING | RESTING |
|---|---|
| FEARFUL | STRIVING |

Which of these times do you live in the most? Why?

How can you move from fear and striving to trust and resting?

# REST

On Sunday, practice a day of Sabbath rest. Throughout the Old Testament, God required Sabbath rest once a week for His people. In addition, there were festival seasons of rest and even a required year of rest. It was an exercise in trust—believing and knowing that it is ultimately God who provides.

Needing rest evidences our limitations. Yet even our limitless God modeled Sabbath rest after creation. Rest is also a gift, a joy, a time to be fully present and to reflect and enjoy the work of our hands and the people God has placed in our lives.

## SUGGESTIONS AS YOU PREPARE FOR A DAY OF REST:

- Lay out some books to read and peruse, along with a journal to jot notes in.
- Do not use technology.
- Prepare the food you and/or your family will need ahead of time.
- Tidy your house to be free of distractions.
- Prepare the people in your life to join you or to respect this time.
- Prepare a playlist of music for your home or Sabbath space.

Now, rest and enjoy.

Enjoy God's presence through prayer, praise, and worship (both private and corporate).

Enjoy your community.

Enjoy and reflect on God's abundance in your life.

## CONSIDER

In what ways is your soul striving? List situations or areas in your life you are trying to control or are worried about. Then next to each fear or worry write what God would say to you about His love for you and His control over every circumstance. Choose Scriptures or just write what you know to be true of Him from your understanding of the Scripture.

| MY FEARS & WORRIES | GOD'S WORDS TO ME |
| --- | --- |
|  |  |

# TRUST

Our ability to enjoy life and find time for our souls to rest is directly related to our trust in God. We often strive because we think we are necessary to God's plans. However, God does not need us, but chooses to be in relationship with us and use us for His purpose. And He built us finite, limited, and unable to work well without rest.

Create a vision of rest for yourself and your family. Write out a plan for regular patterns of rest and trust.

Some things to consider in your plan:

- technology rest

- rest from people outside your home

- rest from work and chores

- books to read

- activities that help your soul to rest

# CONCLUSION

I am falling more in love with Jesus every day of this study. I love how He so desperately wants us to hear that He is enough, that He is better than this world, that He has plans for His people. Our God holds storehouses of joy and rest and hope and everything our souls are striving for, we just have to go to Him for it.

And then you see all the same lies we believe cluttering the lives of others He is trying to persuade.

They ask things like, "What must we do, to be doing the works of God?" (John 6:28, ESV). They choose striving because they think that's what God wants from them. All the while, Jesus knows the way He offers is freedom from that striving, but He also knows most of them won't choose that freedom.

The work is faith. And the irony of that statement is that faith isn't work; faith is resting in God to save, to move, to provide, to change our hearts and anyone else's we might love. Like Andrew, we bring what we have, even though it is insufficient, and we watch our Father God move into our insufficiency with His gracious abundance.

# SEE ::

---

Watch video session 4 now.

Use streaming code on inside cover or DVD.

# RISK ::
## THE END OF PASSIVITY
# 5

When my oldest child, Conner, was two years old I accidentally locked him in my car while it was running.

I know. I know.

I mean, I don't know. I remember the whole thing vividly except the part about how on earth I got out of my car and left it running and how my car became locked while it was running.

Not my best moment. I panicked and there seemed no quick, obvious solution. If I called a locksmith or my husband for my extra keys, Conner could be out of his seat and driving into a wall by the time they arrived.

So I decided I, myself, would lead my son to freedom.

He already knew how to crawl out of his car seat; the first step was already happening. However, he realized pretty quickly I was not able to get to him and started to cry. But he was loose, and after a few moments, he decided exploring the car was better than crying. Of course, I could barely breathe. I began yelling and pointing to the lock, mimicking in the air how to pull the lock up. I must have looked like a fool. Several new parking lot friends gathered and joined in the fun. We were all yelling and mimicking unlocking the door together.

In this moment, my towheaded toddler was at the window watching the show and laughing at all of us. Then, almost like he'd known all along exactly what we wanted him to do, he unlocked the door.

Why am I telling you this story? Because the image of our frantic attempts to get Conner to unlock the door came to mind as I studied the passage you are about to read. While we are trapped in our brokenness and sin, Jesus is waving His arms and showing us the way to freedom, to healing. Of course, He is a bit less hysterical about it.

# STUDY ::

Read JOHN 9

# CULTURAL CONTEXT

Sabbath law was clearly defined in Exodus. However, many other laws concerning the Sabbath had been added by the Pharisees and other religious leaders. In this story, Jesus throwing dirt and spit together would have been considered the work of kneading dirt, thus breaking Sabbath.

# RESPOND

What details do you notice about Jesus' interaction with the blind man?

How did the blind man respond to his healing?

How did the Pharisees respond to the healing?

Why was dealing with Jesus so difficult for them?

What do you think Jesus wants us to understand by His healing on the Sabbath?

In verse 39, Jesus says that many who claim to see are in fact blind and many who have never seen will see.

Here is the verse from The Message:

Jesus then said, "I came into the world to bring everything into the clear light of day, making all the distinctions clear, so that those who have never seen will see, and those who have made a great pretense of seeing will be exposed as blind."

**JOHN 9:39, MSG**

Review John 9 and describe the difference between the blindness and the sight the healed man and the Pharisees experienced:

HEALED MAN

Describe his blindness:

Describe his sight:

PHARISEES

Describe their blindness:

Describe their sight:

## GUTS

What if I told you that to really be free, to enjoy God, to fulfill your purpose here on earth, you must willingly RISK for the glory of God?

Would you search for a text that supports that supposition? Fair.

Here is one of many passages that does so.

> The kingdom of heaven is like treasure hidden in a field, which a man found and covered up. Then in his joy he goes and sells all that he has and buys that field.
>
> **MATTHEW 13:44, ESV**

Jesus said that one who enters the kingdom is like a man who found treasure in a field. The man believed the treasure was worth selling everything he owned. He believed the reward was worth the risk. It took guts to make that call.

It took guts for the blind man to wander down to the water believing what Jesus said would work.

It took guts for Jesus to ignore man-made religious laws to pursue the freedom and healing of one.

It takes guts for us to leave the lies and chains and sin and believe there is something better, something worth losing everything here to obtain.

## Jesus pressed people.

He continually pressed them out of their comfortable lives, cultural expectations, predictable scenarios into freedom, healing, fullness, abundance, joy.

That's the way the Spirit moves.

That's the life God is calling us to.

Can you imagine the hope this life-long blind man had to risk to walk down to the water and wash his eyes? Imagine what he thought to himself as he walked.

## What would you have been thinking?

Can you imagine the respect and approval Jesus was risking as He chose to heal the blind man on the Sabbath? He would potentially be shut down as a religious leader. He risked being considered by some now as a sinner. He risked the judgment of not only those who hated Him but potentially those who were following Him.

Of course, Jesus risked very intentionally, and He knew it was worth it.

## But we know it is worth it, too.

WHO ARE YOU, LORD?    **&**    WHAT DO YOU WANT FOR ME?

*Read Acts 20:22–24. In light of what you read, answer the questions above.*

# DIGGING DEEPER *(OPTIONAL)*

This year I visited Jerusalem for the first time. It's a bustling, exciting city, except on the Shabbat (Sabbath). On that day it's a ghost town. Every store closes down. No one is out. No one is walking around. During Jesus' day, the rules about the Sabbath were even more strict. We have record of a story from two hundred years earlier, when a thousand Jews refused to defend themselves from an attack by the Greek army. They chose to die rather than break the Sabbath.[5]

Both Jesus and the blind man took a lot of risk in John 9. Jesus took a risk by intentionally healing the man on the Sabbath. The man took a risk by obeying Jesus and going to the water to wash his eyes. As the story continued and the man's faith grew, so did his risk-taking.

Read John 9:1. What do you think it would have been like to be blind from birth during this time period? (See 9:8 for a hint.)

How would his life change now that he could see?

Read 9:10–11. How did the healed man refer to Jesus when first questioned by the people?

Read 9:22. What would the Pharisees do to any person who said he or she followed Jesus? What was the man risking?

Read 9:17. How did the formerly blind man refer to Jesus when the Pharisees first questioned him?

Read 9:28–34. When the Pharisees argued with him, how did he respond? What was the consequence?

Read 9:35–39. How did the man respond to Jesus when Jesus found him? Who did the healed man believe Jesus to be?

# SIMPLIFY

One night this week, beginning at sunset, do not use any electricity where you live.

- You will need candles that can be carried.

- You will need to prepare your food in advance.

- Phones will need to be charged earlier that day, but turned off for the evening.

## IDEAS OF HOW TO SPEND THE TIME:

- Make s'mores using the candles or in a fireplace.

- Read by candlelight.

- Play games by candlelight.

- Initiate deep conversations.

- Look at the stars.

It's vulnerable and simple and beautiful to just turn everything off, isn't it?

# RISK

People are people are people.

We just aren't that different. If you seek to find common ground, you always will.

*Choose to do one or both of these ideas:*

☐ Reach out this weekend to someone you may view as different. Go to lunch or get coffee together. Take time to listen and learn from him or her.

☐ Organize a dinner and invite women from different denominations, different ages, different races, different interests. Lay out the conversation cards during your meal and use them for discussion starters.

# CONSIDER

What is the thing you most fear right now? Write it in the space below or draw an image that represents it:

Now consider how your life would be different if that fear were conquered or overcome.

Consider the following ways to face that fear:

- Confess it to a friend.

- Pray about it.

- Memorize Scripture that relates to overcoming it.

- Create an action plan.

Now go do that.

There is no fear in love, but perfect love casts out fear.

**1 JOHN 4:18, ESV**

# CREATE

1. Buy a canvas, a paint set, and paintbrushes. (If you do not have the time or financial resources, gather some simple art supplies from around your house.)

2. Find a quiet spot outside.

3. Sit and observe.

4. Paint or draw something that reminds you of God's beauty.

I know this is going to stretch some of you, which is all the more reason to try it. I warned you this study would push you outside your comfort zones and that we would build new experiences together! Bring your work to class, even if you think it is terrible. It's going to be fun!

# CONCLUSION

I love that so often Jesus is showing us the way to freedom, not just telling us.

Maybe it is because we are more like my toddler son than we wish, a little lost and crawling around distracted. Maybe it is because we learn better when we see love in action, when we see a man walk in sight who was blind, and when we see men who have physical sight, but can't see the truth.

I want to see Jesus.

I want to love Him intimately, not just appear religious. I want to love people enough to lead them to the One who can heal them. I want to want to be healed myself.

I want to sink all I have in the field with the treasure that goes on forever because it is the wisest risk of my life. Is there a risk Christ is calling you to take? There is no more secure venture than risking on an eternal, loving, steadfast God.

## What is holding you back?

# SEE ::

Watch video session 5 now.

Use streaming code on inside cover or DVD.

# HOPE :: 6
## THE END OF FEAR

Many of us began this study because we were so tired from striving. We were afraid we were missing the best parts of our lives toiling and performing, instead of delighting and enjoying the finished work of Christ and the daily power of walking with His Spirit.

Over and over we have seen how much Jesus longs to give us abundant lives and yet today we find ourselves not celebrating at a wedding, but mourning at a funeral. Now I am certain none of you came to this study because you were worried about missing the hardest parts of life—the suffering, the pain, the trials, the conflict, the darkness.

## But what if in trying to miss the hardest parts of life we are also missing the best?

Last week I was given a beautiful and rare gift, a day with a woman who has suffered greatly. She is the wife of a prominent and successful pastor, and together they have faced many trials. But one difficulty they faced is unthinkable: the death of their son. He suffered with depression all of his life and lost his fight with it to suicide a few years ago.

When I sat down with this woman last week, I was losing heart from some of the personal trials our family was facing. But I had not yet been to the place of pain and suffering this mother had. She cried as she talked about the last few years and the unfathomable journey of losing her precious child. She talked about her doubts and her fears and her God with such tenderness and power and honesty it was hard to breathe as I listened. It was all so visceral and raw and fresh.

My own doubts and fears and hurt couldn't hide when confronted with suffering I couldn't stomach or imagine God allowing such a faithful family to endure.

Sometimes when I go there, to the darkest parts of my story or the stories around me, when I glimpse the pain and suffering that our loving God doesn't spare us from, I feel desperately afraid.

I am afraid He isn't good enough.

I am afraid He isn't powerful enough.

I am afraid He doesn't love us enough.

And guess what happens next? I go numb. I pick numb over fear. I pick numb over despair. I pick numb over moving into my own pain or anyone else's.

But again, what if we are missing the very best parts by pushing away the hardest?

Jesus is calling you into the darkest places, because in the darkest places, His love and light burn brightest.

I will not forget this woman's tender words to me as we left each other. She hugged me tightly and said, "Jennie, despite all the hard, Jesus is still worth it."

# STUDY ::

Read JOHN 11

# RESPOND

Why did Jesus wait to go to Lazarus?

What feelings and convictions do you hear in Martha's words in verses 21–22?

How did Jesus respond to Martha?

Describe Mary's faith and posture in verses 28–32? How was it different than Martha's?

How did Jesus respond to Mary?

Why do you think Jesus wept with Mary?

What did Jesus ultimately want for the people He loved (v. 15)?

## WHERE HOPE LIVES

Who in their right mind chooses pain and suffering?

In fact, underlying most decisions we make on an everyday basis is a deep desire to avoid pain and suffering. From using hand sanitizer to meeting a friend for lunch, pain and risk management is a big priority for all of us.

We don't want to get sick. We don't want to feel alone. We don't want to be hungry. We don't even want to eat bad food so we pick a favorite place. Is it wrong to act this way? Actually no, it isn't wrong. It's just human. In fact it isn't only humans; even most animals are built with the same primary goals.

- Avoid pain.

- Avoid suffering.

- Avoid danger.

- Avoid risk.

It is best to understand our resistance.

I believe God is all-powerful and everything Jesus does and says and allows to transpire is for our good and for His glory.

Jesus takes everyone in the John 11 story deep into the dark grave of pain and suffering. He doesn't stop a death of a dearly loved friend, and He doesn't spare those He loves days of agonizing grief and suffering. He could have prevented this entire ordeal, yet He allows it to unfold.

Why? John shared the purpose clearly in verses 4 and 14:

## For our faith and for His glory.

It's obvious Jesus hates death in this passage, and He hates watching those He loves suffer. I spent a bit of time considering (as you probably have also) exactly why Jesus cried. He knew what would happen moments later. You'd think He'd be excited to exercise His power over death and to see His friend.

But He paused and grieved with Mary.

Jesus is obviously complex and there is no way to know all that He was feeling in those moments. But one thing He must have felt was compassion for all that Mary and Martha and all the other humans around Him, whom He deeply loved, couldn't yet see or understand. He alluded to this lack of perspective earlier in the chapter:

> If anyone walks in the day, he does not stumble, because he sees the light of this world. But if anyone walks in the night, he stumbles, because the light is not in him.
>
> **JOHN 11:9–10, ESV**

Perhaps Jesus cried with Mary because, for a moment, He considered what it must be like to stumble in fear in the dark, to not have a clear hope and picture of heaven, and to despair at death. Perhaps it troubled Him because Mary's eyes could not yet see what is waiting for those who believe.

In 1 Corinthians 2:9, Paul stated, "What no eye has seen, nor ear heard, nor the heart of man imagined, what God has prepared for those who love him..." (ESV). However, Jesus' eyes, ears, heart, and imagination have seen.

He knew all that God had prepared, yet He was not going to reveal it on that day. While He might temporarily suspend this day's pain and grief, He knew that suffering and pain remain a part of the human equation. But He was determined to give them the one thing that could transport them to all that was waiting for them:

Faith.

Then Jesus said, "Did I not tell you that if you believe, you will see the glory of God?" So they took away the stone. Then Jesus looked up and said, "Father, I thank you that you have heard me. I knew that you always hear me, but I said this for the benefit of the people standing here, that they may believe that you sent me." When he had said this, Jesus called in a loud voice, "Lazarus, come out!" The dead man came out, his hands and feet wrapped with strips of linen, and a cloth around his face. Jesus said to them, "Take off the grave clothes and let him go." Therefore many of the Jews who had come to visit Mary, and had seen what Jesus did, believed in him.

**JOHN 11:40–45**

Is it conceivable that God may allow temporary suffering to expand our faith? Absolutely. (See Rom. 5:1–5; James. 1:2–4.) Our faith, tried and tested, will lead us to our eternal home where pain and suffering will never touch us again.

But what if the very thing that God is allowing for our good, our faith, our hope, our perseverance, we keep pushing away and avoiding?

We can either move into the suffering within us and around us or we can try to avoid it. But if we choose avoidance, not only will we miss the hard parts but we will miss the best parts, too.

WHO ARE YOU, LORD?  WHAT DO YOU WANT FOR ME?

Read 2 Corinthians 4:16–18. In light of what you read, answer the questions above.

# DIGGING DEEPER *(OPTIONAL)*

JOHN 11:45–12:19

Read 11:45–46. What were the two different ways the people responded to Jesus raising Lazarus from the dead?

Read 11:47–53. At the end of their discussion, what did the Pharisees determine to do in response to Jesus raising a man from the dead?

Read 11:54. Do you think Jesus knew what the Pharisees had decided? How did He respond?

Read 11:55–12:1. What feast were the Pharisees referring to in verse 56?

Read 12:12–16. This passage is often referred to as the triumphal entry or what we celebrate in church as Palm Sunday. What happened at the end of this week (John 19)?

Read 12:17–19. Why did the crowds go out to see Jesus? What was the Pharisees' response?

By healing Lazarus, Jesus knew this would trigger the Pharisees' plot to kill Him. He was headed to the cross. How does this impact the way we read the story in John 11?

# REFLECT

This week we are going to face some of our darkest fears and hurts. I know this is so sacred and tender. I am praying that every single one of you will brave this. I also pray you'd clearly know the presence of the God of all comfort. Know that He stands ready to strengthen your heart, bind your wounds, and carry your burdens.

This week take an hour or two by yourself with a journal and consider these questions.

What are some of your greatest disappointments? Can you see the presence and purpose of Jesus in those moments? Where? How?

What are some of your greatest doubts about God? Have you shared those doubts with Him? What do you think Jesus would say to the doubts?

What are some of your deepest hurts and insecurities? How does Jesus want to meet these needs in your life?

What are you most afraid of? What do you believe Jesus would say to your greatest fear?

# CONNECT

Jesus moved into Mary's hurt. How can you move into someone's hurt this week?

Who in your life is lonely, sick, or suffering?

Can you spend some time with that person this week? If so, don't let your purpose for going be to give advice or fix the situation. Just be there to listen and hurt with him or her.

If you don't have time to be physically present with your friend or family member, could you take a meal or prepare a gift?

If you are blessed to not know anyone in your immediate life who is suffering, visit a local nursing home. Minister to the ladies there with nail polish and lotion. While you paint their nails or give them hand massages, ask them about their lives, using some of the following questions:

- What was your first car?

- What decade of music was your favorite?

- What was your childhood like?

Move into someone's loneliness.

*Answer these questions about your experience:*

What did you learn about suffering?

What did you learn about Jesus?

What did you learn about yourself?

# MEDITATE

*Meditate on this passage from Isaiah. Note the imagery and write what it means to you.*

*Replace your own disappointments or hurts or fears with the imagery mentioned in this passage, if needed. He is making all things new for those who are His.*

"Sing, O barren one, who did not bear; break forth into singing and cry aloud, you who have not been in labor! For the children of the desolate one will be more than the children of her who is married," says the LORD. "Enlarge the place of your tent, and let the curtains of your habitations be stretched out; do not hold back; lengthen your cords and strengthen your stakes. For you will spread abroad to the right and to the left, and your offspring will possess the nations and will people the desolate cities. Fear not, for you will not be ashamed; be not confounded, for you will not be disgraced; for you will forget the shame of your youth, and the reproach of your widowhood you will remember no more. For your Maker is your husband, the LORD of hosts is his name; and the Holy One of Israel is your Redeemer, the God of the whole earth he is called. For the LORD has called you like a wife deserted and grieved in spirit, like a wife of youth when she is cast off, says your God. For a brief moment I deserted you, but with great compassion I will gather you. In overflowing anger for a moment I hid my face from you, but with everlasting love I will have compassion on you," says the

LORD, your Redeemer. "This is like the days of Noah to me: as I swore that the waters of Noah should no more go over the earth, so I have sworn that I will not be angry with you, and will not rebuke you. For the mountains may depart and the hills be removed, but my steadfast love shall not depart from you, and my covenant of peace shall not be removed," says the LORD, who has compassion on you. "O afflicted one, storm-tossed and not comforted, behold, I will set your stones in antimony, and lay your foundations with sapphires. I will make your pinnacles of agate, your gates of carbuncles, and all your wall of precious stones. All your children shall be taught by the LORD, and great shall be the peace of your children. In righteousness you shall be established; you shall be far from oppression, for you shall not fear; and from terror, for it shall not come near you. If anyone stirs up strife, it is not from me; whoever stirs up strife with you shall fall because of you. Behold, I have created the smith who blows the fire of coals and produces a weapon for its purpose. I have also created the ravager to destroy; no weapon that is fashioned against you shall succeed, and you shall refute every tongue that rises against you in judgment. This is the heritage of the servants of the LORD and their vindication from me, declares the LORD."

**ISAIAH 54,ESV**

Underline the promises from God in this passage.

Describe what the promises in this passage mean to you.

# RISK

Okay friends, this is down-and-dirty brave work.

As we talked about earlier in this study, often we avoid our doubts and hurts. This experience will help you bring those things to light. This week, sit down with some trusted friends or family members and permit them to ask you the following questions.

What hurt are you holding onto? Why?

How do you think Jesus feels about your pain or disappointment?

Is there value in going to difficult places? If so, what is it?

How have you seen Jesus redeem some of your
dark times?

How has that strengthened your hope and trust in Him?

Is there any other hurt or disappointment you are avoiding?
If so, what is it?

How can I love you well right now?

# CONCLUSION

My son Cooper has experienced more loss and suffering at the age of seven than most people will in their lifetimes. Because of the loss of both of his biological parents, his first four crucial years of life were spent in a third-world orphanage without enough love, food, or attention. He spent one of those years in leg casts and braces.

Yet you have never met a kid so full of life and joy. Is the joy my son lives with a result of the suffering he has faced? I don't know. But I do know that rather than hiding all that pain and all those memories deep inside, my son talks about it. He opens up about his sadness and hurt all the time.

Sometimes out of the blue he looks at me and says, "Why would my first mommy leave me?"

He goes there. It is awful and hard but I love that he processes his pain. He doesn't ignore it or numb it. He's learned he can face the pain because there is life, joy, and healing in this safe place with us. And while we can't ever take away the pain, we are there to comfort him in it.

We don't have to be afraid to go into the darkest grave if Jesus is in it with us. And He is.

# SEE ::

Watch video session 6 now.

Use streaming code on inside cover or DVD.

# GRACE :: 7
## THE END OF SHAME

Not long ago, I was teaching the passage we are about to study to a room full of pastor's wives and ministry leaders. I sensed brokenness in the room. I sensed bondage that perhaps had been holding some of them for decades. At the conclusion of the talk, I hadn't planned on doing this, but I asked them to stand up and name the sin that they were afraid to confess. I went first. "My sin is that I try to find my worth in my abilities and how I am measuring up to God and people, rather than knowing that my identity, given to me by Christ, is unchangeable, immovable, completely secure."

It was quiet, and then after about 30 silent seconds women began standing up and speaking up. Women who lead their churches, their Bible studies, and their friends, began to stand up so fast they were all speaking over each other.

Honestly, I couldn't hear all of their responses. There were so many and they came so fast.

But the room shifted.

I don't know if it was the freedom they all felt from saying their sin out loud, or the power of hearing everyone else fighting their sin, but that room of faithful women who loved Jesus went from leaders to warriors that day. Grace filled that room, and the cold refreshing streams of water we all were so desperate for flooded the place. And we all drank deeply from it.

We are afraid of being caught. But, because of Jesus, being caught is one of the greatest gifts He gives us. It is the moment we start to get free. It is the moment we can finally receive grace.

# STUDY ::

Read JOHN 13

## CULTURAL CONTEXT

In Jesus' day, it was customary to offer your guests a basin of water for their feet. But guests were usually expected to wash their own feet. Washing someone else's feet was a task reserved for only the lowest ranking servants.

## RESPOND

Describe Peter's reaction to Jesus' humble act.

Why do you think Jesus insisted on Peter receiving this cleansing?

What was Jesus hoping that His men understood by this act?

> A new commandment I give to you, that you love one
> another: just as I have loved you, you also are to love one
> another. By this all people will know that you are my disciples,
> if you have love for one another.
>
> **JOHN 13:34–35, ESV**

Describe the kind of love Jesus is calling us to in this chapter.

Why is Jesus so adamantly demonstrating and calling us to
this kind of love (see v. 35)?

## HUMILITY

The Christian life can be summed up in these three words that Jesus used often:

## Repent and believe.

Turn from your sin and believe the truth of God.

This will take humility.

In my experience, the word *humility* usually involves a bit of humiliation. Every time that I am honest about my struggles and honest about my sin and honest about my pride and honest about the mistakes that I've made and honest about the sin in my soul, I find it humiliating.

I let that humiliation flood over me. It leads to repentance. Followed by forgiveness. The shame that I'd been feeling that inevitably had affected me and everyone around me is washed away by the waves of grace.

This grace brings connection again. It is a deep, honest, sincere in-my-soul kind of connection with God, because I need Him again and I'm close to Him again and we're right.

But it costs me something to get there.

It's our human nature to pull back our dirty foot. If the goal of our lives is intimacy with Jesus, then the pathway to that intimacy is vulnerably needing Him—bringing Him the things we most want to hide from Him. The disciples fought for positions, they fought to be the greatest, they fought to perform, they fought to be honored. They'd hidden their weakness and pretended to be more than they were.

But Jesus' identity drove His humility. He wasn't grasping for anything—He had nothing to prove. He was secure enough to face humiliation for these men, and eventually for the whole world, hours later on a cross.

True faith leads us to repentance. The power of repentance is the death it contains. Freedom doesn't come without death. Happiness doesn't come without dirt. And singing only comes after the mourning.

The upper room is the story of this backward way.

We risk our dirt because Jesus has the power to wash it and we no longer want to be in bondage to it. We want to see revival happen in our places; we want to see God move in the souls of people around us. Yes? We want that.

It starts with us. If we don't experience His forgiveness and His grace on a regular basis, then how could we give away His forgiveness and grace to anybody else?

Jesus moved into the dirt of His people, and His people let Him. Moving into our dirt and the dirt of others is costly and difficult, but it is where we were made to be. It's not because there is life in the mess. It's because there is healing available to anyone who will unveil their mess.

Jesus has the power and authority to cleanse us.

## What keeps you from being wholly honest with God about your dirt?

I picture Peter pulling back his dirty feet from Jesus, not wanting to receive what he most needed. Jesus' response: "If I do not wash you, you have no share with me" (v. 8, ESV).

What I love about our generation is that we are likely to name our junk. But are we willing to repent from it? There is nothing holy about authenticity without repentance. Authenticity without repentance is narcissism. Authenticity is the necessary soil for repentance, but if healing comes from Jesus, then confession is only the first step.

Grieving and leaving our sin is the next one.

## What makes us clean?
## His blood makes us clean.

Jesus was clear, only those who accept His cleansing will become a part of Him. Only those who are willing to confess, repent, expose their sin, and receive His forgiveness will have eternal life.

And it's also important, as James tells us, that we confess to each other, not the dirty details of our sin, but the fact of them (James 5:16). All of us have dirty feet. All of us are frail. All of us struggle. All of us need Jesus. Let's expose the depth of our sin to the Savior and our struggle with it to each other that we might be truly known and walk in freedom together.

WHO ARE YOU, LORD? & WHAT DO YOU WANT FOR ME?

Read 1 John 1:5–10. In light of what you read, answer the questions above.

# DIGGING DEEPER (OPTIONAL)

Read John 1:26–27. Even though John the Baptist wasn't describing washing feet, he described a similarly humble task reserved for slaves. What did he understand about Jesus from the start that the disciples didn't understand until later?

Read Luke 22:24. This verse provides more context to what occurred just before the meal. What were the disciples doing?

Read John 13:1–7. What prompted Jesus to get up from the table?

In verse 7, what did Jesus tell Peter? What do you think Jesus meant by "but later you will understand"?

Read John 13:12–17. What was the meaning of the foot washing and what was Jesus' challenge?

Read Philippians 2:5–11. Jesus knew what would take place shortly after He washed His disciples' feet. Imagine what Jesus was thinking as He held their feet and washed the dirt off.

Read 1 Peter 2:21–24. These are Peter's own words after the cross and resurrection. Now that Peter fully understood who Jesus was, how do you think he looked back on Jesus washing his feet?

# BE

Spend some time connecting with Jesus today. Read the following passage and be still for 5–10 minutes. Listen to what Jesus wants to say to you through His Word.

> Let us therefore strive to enter that rest, so that no one may fall by the same sort of disobedience. For the word of God is living and active, sharper than any two-edged sword, piercing to the division of soul and of spirit, of joints and of marrow, and discerning the thoughts and intentions of the heart. And no creature is hidden from his sight, but all are naked and exposed to the eyes of him to whom we must give account.
>
> Since then we have a great high priest who has passed through the heavens, Jesus, the Son of God, let us hold fast our confession. For we do not have a high priest who is unable to sympathize with our weaknesses, but one who in every respect has been tempted as we are, yet without sin. Let us then with confidence draw near to the throne of grace, that we may receive mercy and find grace to help in time of need.
>
> **HEBREWS 4:11–16, ESV**

Does this passage comfort you? Challenge you? Frighten you?

Did anything come to mind that you need to confess before God?

Take time now to draw near to the throne with confidence to confess your sin, lay down your burden, and cry out for help.

# CREATE

When you consider risking being wholly transparent with someone, what keeps you from it?

Draw an image that represents your feelings about it here.

What practical step are you going to take today to move into transparency with someone close to you?

# CONFESS

For all have sinned and fall short of the glory of God.

**ROMANS 3:23**

Read this beautiful puritan prayer from *Valley of Vision* as you lay out your confession before Jesus.

*Lord Jesus,*
*give me a deeper repentance,*
*a horror of sin,*
*a dread of its approach.*
*Help me chastely to flee it*
*and jealously to resolve that my heart shall be thine alone.*
*Give me a deeper trust,*
*that I may lose myself to find myself in thee,*
*the ground of my rest,*
*the spring of my being.*
*Give me a deeper knowledge of thyself*
*as Saviour, Master, Lord, and King.*
*Give me deeper power in private prayer,*
*more sweetness in thy Word,*
*more steadfast grip on its truth.*
*Give me deeper holiness in speech, thought, action,*
*and let me not seek moral virtue apart from thee.*[6]

Is there any sin in your past that you have not confessed or dealt with? Are there strongholds currently in your life? If so, write your own prayer of repentance.

# IMAGINE

One of the greatest thirsts we all have is for grace. Dream about how you could pour the grace you so richly enjoy on someone else today.

Who is someone that needs to be refreshed by the grace of the Lord?

What creative thing could you do for someone that would bless them and cause them to feel loved? Jesus knelt and washed His men's feet with cool water. What can you do today to serve someone?

# CONCLUSION

What Peter did not know is that later that night, fulfilling Jesus' prophecy (John 13:36–38), he would deny Christ three times.

How quickly the need for cleansing arises in our lives.

We barely even know how much we need grace. We are ignorant or dismissive of what we are capable of. However, we stand in need of forgiveness. I need this forgiveness today. You need this forgiveness today. Jesus has it and is offering it to you right now.

*I wash your pride that thinks that I need you.*
*I wash your doubt that you think I can't handle.*
*I wash your fear that stops you.*
*I wash your shame that makes you hide.*
*I wash your independence that makes you think you don't need Me.*
*I wash your performance that you think you must produce.*
*I wash your betrayal that haunts you.*
*I wash your pride that thinks you are above needing forgiveness.*
*I wash your striving for your own name.*
*I wash your love for your own honor.*
*I wash your mistakes that you cannot name.*
*I wash your anger that sneaks out sometimes.*
*I wash your feet and set them on a single path.*

It is a single path of service, a path of love, a path of rejection, a path of suffering, a path of joy, a path of setting people free. Let's not miss it. It feels good to be free.

# SEE ::

Watch video session 7 now.

Use streaming code on inside cover or DVD.

# CALLED :: 8
## THE END OF EMPTINESS

We began this journey with great hopes of experiencing lives more awakened, more full, more focused, more connected, more present, more joy-filled. I have journeyed with you and I can honestly say I feel all of that. This journey into Jesus' life and words has changed me.

It wasn't the journey I had planned when I began. It was better and messier and more difficult. But isn't that how it goes?

One of my dear friends has brought my family dinner once a week for the past several weeks because she feels this is what God wants her to do right now. We aren't sick. We're not walking through a difficult time. So of course I panic and resist every time. I hate to receive. I feel so undeserving. But when I resist my friend says, "This isn't about you. This is me obeying God, Jennie. So, tough."

What I haven't told her for all of these weeks is that I cry every time she brings me food. It feels like the kindest gift to me. It just feels like God's surprising, beautiful, extravagant love to me. What if we all just did the thing God put in us to do every day? If that happened, I have a feeling we could end up making the whole world feel the surprising, beautiful, extravagant love of our God. There are an awful lot of us. Perhaps we could at least make a dent.

I believe that is what this journey was. And I didn't see it coming.

It has been God showing me over and over that His love is unending and extravagant. He isn't waiting for me to achieve; He is waiting for me to receive.

He desperately wants me to feel loved and to move and breathe and connect and love out of that love. We are about to see how Jesus creatively connected to His men just before He completed His work on earth. He didn't require perfection or striving. He just issued them beautiful rhythms of grace that caused them to rest and enjoy God. Then, their obedience flowed out of a relationship, out of being loved.

# STUDY ::

Read JOHN 21

# CULTURAL CONTEXT

Jesus had been resurrected and had already appeared twice to His disciples (John 20:19,26). This was one of their last times together before He ascended to heaven. It was the first time Peter and Jesus addressed Peter's denial that came just after Jesus washed Peter's feet.

# RESPOND

Describe the apostles' fishing experience prior to Jesus appearing on shore.

What was different after Jesus appeared?

Describe Peter's response to seeing Jesus.

Why do you think Peter responded this way?

What did Jesus provide for His disciples that morning?

What do you think He wanted from them in that moment?

What do you think He wants from you in this moment?

## FREE TO LOVE GOD

God's pattern throughout the Old and New Testament is to set His people free, but it was always for a single purpose. In Exodus, He sent Moses to set His people free so that they could worship God (Ex. 9:1).

We are forgiven and set free so that we can worship and enjoy our God forever. This is what we were designed to do. We place expectations on ourselves of what we could, would, and should do for God if we really had our act together. But our expectations are not necessarily His. Jesus lived with one mission: to do the will of His Father. He calls us to do the same. It begins with loving God, then loving others.

We sometimes complicate God and all He wants from us or for us. But He just wants us.

The word *holy* means to be set apart for God, to be, as it were, exclusively His. It's easy to feel burdened by the importance and urgency of the mission of God. To some degree that is not all bad. However, the mission of God is so simple: to love God with all of our hearts, minds, souls, and strength, and to love our neighbors as ourselves.

You might ask, *But what about the Great Commission? Isn't our mission to be making disciples?* I contend that if we truly love God and truly love our neighbor, then we will desperately want them to know Him. Therefore, we will make disciples.

In the Old Testament there was a concentrated focus on holiness. Holy sacrifices, holy days, holy seasons, and holy food. One of the religious codes was keeping holy instruments in the temple. What made any of these things holy was that they were set apart by God, for God's purpose. God blessed the Sabbath and made it holy (Ex. 20:8–11). He set it apart for His purpose—for us to be with Him.

And I believe that is the point here—that we exist for one solitary purpose: to love God with all of us and in turn show His grand love to everyone He puts in our paths.

But too often we bow to the pressure of needing to show God's love before we have even experienced it. We move out into the work before the relationship. We start with "doing" for Him instead of starting with "being" with Him. In John 21, when the disciples got to shore, Jesus didn't immediately give them marching orders. He cooked them breakfast. They ate. Talked. Perhaps laughed and told stories. The plans He had for them would come later. After the meal, He would call Peter to feed His sheep. Days later He would commission all of them to make disciples (Matt. 28:19–20). But first they had breakfast.

I believe that is why I was so weary as I began this journey. I was trying to prove myself, rather than enjoy Jesus who has already proven everything for me.

I was urgently trying to produce fruit instead of abiding in God's love and enjoying it wholly, single-mindedly, without distraction.

What does it look like for you to be *holy*—single-minded, exclusively belonging to God?

How would your life be different if your focus was first on belonging to God, being with God, loving God?

What keeps you from that life?

What if that was your only goal walking away from this study? No other mission but to love God exclusively and completely with all that you are? What would change?

WHO ARE YOU, LORD? & WHAT DO YOU WANT FOR ME?

Read 2 Corinthians 5:17–21. In light of what you read, answer the questions above.

# DIGGING DEEPER *(OPTIONAL)*

Read John 21:3. What did Peter and the disciples with him decide to do? What was the result of their labor?

Read John 21:4–6. What did Jesus tell the disciples to do? What was the result?

Think back to our study of John 6:1–15. What do you think the disciples thought of when their nets were suddenly filled with fish? What was the result of their obedience in both stories?

Read John 21:7. What was Peter's response? Why do you think he responded that way?

Read John 13:36–38. How many times did Jesus say Peter would betray Him?

Read John 18:15–18. What does the girl ask Peter? What does he say? What is he standing next to when this happens?

Read John 21:9. What had Jesus prepared for the disciples? What items were there? What did Jesus use to cook the fish?

Read John 21:15–19. What did Jesus ask Peter? How many times did He ask him? Why do you think He asked him this specific number of times?

Read the following passages and note how Peter fulfilled the challenge Jesus gave to him.

Acts 2:14–41

Acts 3:1–10

Acts 3:11–26

Acts 10:1–47

# DREAM

Where could you display God's extravagant love around you? Dream a little.

What needs do you see around you?

What nudge do you feel from God concerning these needs? Which one may He be wanting you to meet (even if it seems small)?

What is keeping you from responding?

# REFLECT

What have you learned about yourself in these weeks?

What have you learned about Jesus?

How has the Holy Spirit convicted you about the way you are living?

What is now your vision for your life, your friends, and your family?

# VISION

Many years ago, as I was just beginning my writing ministry, I would lose focus. I would often find myself wondering: "What am I doing and why?" Because, like everything God calls us to, His growing mission for my life was becoming more and more costly. I needed some anchor to return to when it all felt out of control.

So I spent time praying and talking with some trusted mentors and friends. One of them suggested I write a life mission statement. I did, and it has gone on to serve as a reminder, a compass, and a kick in the pants when I need it.

My mission statement:

## Be free and set others free.

Of course that mission is accomplished only through Christ's redemptive power and love.

Your mission statement should be based on your passions and what you hope people will say about you when you are gone. Look over Jesus' prayer in John 17 and consider what it is God has called you to and what He has done already through your life for the good of others and His glory.

*Here are some things to consider as you work on this statement:*

- Pray and read Scripture. You want your statement to reflect God's heart and purpose.

- Consider your gifts and passions.

- Think about your legacy. How do you want people to remember you when you're gone?

- Reflect on how God has already worked in and through you.

- Seek the counsel and observations of trusted, godly friends. How have they seen God work through you?

So it's your turn. Write a mission statement for your life.

# GATHER

Fire up the grill, put the burgers and dogs on, or gather family and/or close friends again around the fire pit. Spend time around the table or fire discussing some of the following questions:

Do you ever find yourself letting doing things *for* God be more important than being *with* God?

What is your priority mission?

Do you ever feel like you've let God down? Explain.

# CONCLUSION

I truly believe as we lean more and more into Christ's work for us and less on our own work, the abundant, awakened, connected life we all crave grows around us. And as we do, we will learn joy and will choose God and His will for our lives over our comfort.

However, whenever there is God in great measure, there is darkness in great measure trying to extinguish the light. This is an old war, fought by believers for centuries.

Rather than become numb and miss it, let's step up to our time in history and get in on the fight. I believe we are ready to wake up. I believe we are craving more of God, no matter the cost. I have seen it in your eyes.

The need for God in this world is clear and pervasive. I believe Jesus wants to use this project to awaken His people and have us take our place in the greater story. I want less days of coping and more days of fighting for God's glory and the good of people.

I know I am not alone.

Friends, let's do this. Let's live this.

What are you leaving behind?

What are you moving toward?

# SEE ::

Watch video session 8 now.

Use streaming code on inside cover or DVD.

# COMMISSIONING

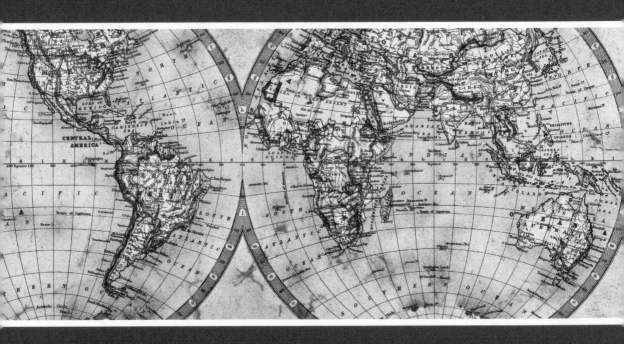

We are a generation of women who desire to be brave.

May our bravery lead us to sacrificial obedience.

May heaven become more real than earth.

May we see God, really see Him. And then care more about what He thinks than any other person on earth.

May we go to war against bondage that has controlled us and kept us from living the lives that we were meant to live.

May we crave freedom for God's people.

May the state of our hearts become more concerning to us than our reputations.

May our generation live knowing God is real.

May the religious come back to Jesus.

May the faithless find Him safe to consider.

May we see that heaven is coming and that we have a mission.

I want to see in my lifetime a generation of un-numb, un-stuck, focused missionaries, empowered by the Spirit building the kingdom of God together.

# LEADER'S GUIDE

Dear leader,

Your willingness to invest truth in the lives of women around you is the greatest act of obedience to Jesus. Right before Jesus ascended to heaven He said to those whom He had spent years investing into, "All authority in heaven and on earth has been given to me. Therefore go and make disciples of all nations, baptizing them in the name of the Father and of the Son and of the Holy Spirit, and teaching them to obey everything I have commanded you. And surely I am with you always, to the very end of the age" (Matt. 28:18–20).

Make disciples—baptize, teach them to obey—and then finally He says, "I am with you."

Leadership in any form should humble us and make us sober that we are giving people God. It is no small task and we are certain, every one of us, to do that imperfectly. However, God is with us and as we seek to honor Him and to love and invest His Word in those around us, He will move and change lives.

Thank you for partnering with me to cause growth and life change in women. It is my greatest privilege to enter this sacred work with you. My prayers are with you.

Grateful,

Jennie

# PREPARING YOURSELF TO LEAD

## 1. PRAY

Pray for yourself: Pray that you will be led by the Spirit. Pray that you would lead with wisdom, compassion, discernment, and urgency. Pray fervently and continuously.

Pray for your women that they would:

- know they don't have to prove themselves, but that Jesus has proven everything;

- have hearts that are teachable and moldable;

- be transformed by God's Word and His Spirit.

## 2. LEAN ON GOD

Don't lead this Bible study in your own power. Allow the Holy Spirit to lead every moment—your preparation, your facilitation, your follow-up.

Don't just teach what's on the page. Allow the Spirit freedom to work outside the boundaries of your plan and agenda.

Depend on God for the results. Don't try to manufacture moments or experiences. Keep in mind your responsibility is to be obedient and faithful to teach the Word. The results are left to God.

Teach out of the overflow of your own walk with God. You can't pour out much truth from an empty pitcher. Spend time daily with the Savior in an intimate love relationship with Him. Let Him pour into you before you pour out on others.

## 3. BE VULNERABLE

There will be times you will need to open up and share your life. This will help others feel safe to share. But don't feel like you have to share every detail. You don't. Share what is necessary, guided by the Holy Spirit.

## 4. LISTEN, BUT ALSO LEAD

Allow women to share their struggles and do your best not to interrupt. However, you will need to guide the conversation. You will need to include all women in the discussion. You will need to continue to steer the conversation back to the truth of God's Word.

## 5. MODEL TRUST

Don't be a "do as I say" leader. Be the example. Apply what you have learned and are learning through the study.

# THE STUDY: SESSION TOOLS AND FORMAT

*Nothing to Prove* is designed to work in various types of venues and locations, including homes, dorm rooms, work places, or churches. Whether you find yourself leading a large group of women at church or a few neighbors in your home, the study is designed for small groups of women to share and process truth. I suggest a maximum number of eight in your group. If you are leading a large group at church, divide into smaller groups and enlist women to lead each small group.

## WHAT'S IN THE BOX:

STUDY. One copy of the Bible study guide. Streaming video access code is included with each study guide on the inside front cover.

SEE. Eight sessions of video teaching available on DVD or streaming using the access code printed on the inside cover of study guide.

ASK. One set of Conversation Cards.

# SESSION TOOLS AND HOW TO USE THEM

### STUDY.

Every participant will need a Bible study guide. Distribute the books at your first group meeting and walk participants through them. Point out the weekly Study section, followed by the four application Experiences. The Study and the Experiences can be completed in one sitting or spaced throughout the week. The lessons in the book (except for the Introduction lesson) should be completed between group meetings.

The lessons are interactive, designed to help women study Scripture for themselves and apply it to their lives. The Experiences in the Bible study guide will provide creative options for applying Scripture. Some of these Experiences may push the women outside their comfort zones. Encourage them to be brave and tackle the challenge. Make sure to discuss the Experiences at each group meeting.

### SEE.

Watch the short, engaging video teaching to introduce the lesson, set the tone for your time together, and challenge women to apply Scripture. If your group members want to take notes, encourage them to use the "Notes" page opposite each SEE:: title page. Each study guide includes a personal access code to Streaming Video on the inside front cover. This is perfect for women who miss a group gathering, want to re-watch any of the video teaching, or if your group needs to meet on shortened time.

## ASK.

The Conversation Cards provide a unique way to jump-start honest discussion. Each week's cards are labeled with the appropriate lesson title and can be used after the video or teaching time. The following is a suggested step-by-step way to use the cards:

1. Lay out the cards for the specific week with the questions facing up.

2. Direct each woman to take a card.

3. Go over the Ground Rules each week. (Ground Rules are found on page 5 and on the back of the Instruction card.)

4. Begin by laying out the Scripture Card for that specific lesson.

5. Allow each woman to ask the question on the card she selected. Provide adequate time for women to respond to the question.

Don't feel pressured to read and answer each question. Be sensitive to the leading of the Holy Spirit and your time constraints.

## NOTE.

Make use of this leader's guide to facilitate a great Bible study experience for your group. It will help you point women to the overarching theme for each lesson and will give you specific suggestions on how to share the truth and foster discussion.

# SESSION FORMAT

The eight-week study is designed to go deep very quickly, so it's flexible
when considering the length of your group sessions. It can be led in a church
spread out over a couple of hours, or in a break room over a one-hour lunch.
However, the more time you can allow for discussion, the better. When the
group is given deep questions and space to reflect and respond, you'll be
surprised by the depth and beauty of the conversations.

You will be the best judge of what time and format works for your group.
However, here is a suggested schedule for each group meeting.

## 1. OPEN - *PERSONAL STUDY DISCUSSION (15–35 MINUTES)*

After a warm welcome and opening prayer, provide time for the women to
share and discuss their personal reflections from the study of Scripture
and the Experiences. If you have more than eight in your group, break into
smaller groups for this discussion.

## 2. WATCH - *VIDEO TEACHING (10–15 MINUTES)*

Use the video to lay the foundation for the week's lesson and transition to
the Conversation Cards. Feel free to provide supplemental teaching for your
group. We recommend that you begin with your personal study discussion,
then play the video.

## 3. ASK - *CONVERSATION CARDS (25–75 MINUTES)*

Allow time for women to ask and discuss the question on each card. If you
need an extra set of cards, they are available for purchase from your favorite
online retailer.

## 4. CLOSE - *CLOSING ACTIVITY (5–10 MINUTES)*

We have provided you with an optional activity you can use to close each
session.

# TIPS FOR LEADING YOUR GROUP

Always encourage the group members to abide by the following Ground Rules for discussion. These rules can be found below, on the back of the Instruction Card, and on page 6 in this Bible study book.

## BE CONCISE

Share your answers to the questions while protecting others' time for sharing. Be considerate. Don't be afraid to share with the group, but try not to dominate the conversation.

## KEEP GROUP MEMBERS' STORIES CONFIDENTIAL

Your group members will want to share sensitive and personal information with you, not with your husband or other friends. Protect each other by not allowing anything shared in the group to leave the group.

## RELY ON SCRIPTURE FOR TRUTH

Conventional, worldly wisdom has value, but it is not absolute truth. Only Scripture provides that. In your times of discussion, be careful not to equate good advice with God's Truth.

## NO COUNSELING

Work together to protect the group by not directing all attention on solving one person's problem. This is the place for confessing and discovery and applying truth together as a group. However, at times a member may need to dig even deeper with an outside counselor or talk with a friend outside of small group time. If that is you, don't be afraid to ask for help, or be sure and follow up with a member of the group.

# WHEN TO REFER

Some of the women in your group may be dealing with issues beyond your ability to help. If you sense that a woman may need more extensive help, refer her to speak with your pastor or a trained Christian counselor. Maintain the relationship and follow up with her to make sure she is getting the care needed. You or someone else in your group may need to walk with her through this season of her life. As we have said many times, be sensitive to the Holy Spirit's leading as you love and offer hope to the women in your group.

# TYPES OF LEARNERS

Hopefully, you will be blessed to be leading this study with a group diverse in age, experience, and style. While the benefits of coming together as a diverse group to discuss God outweigh the challenges by a mile, there are often distinctions in learning styles. Just be aware and consider some of the differences in two types of learning styles that may be represented. (These are obviously generalizations, and each woman as an individual will expressher own unique communication style, but typically these are common characteristics.)

## EXPERIENTIAL LEARNERS

There are women who are more transparent, don't like anything cheesy, want to go deep quickly, and are passionate. Make a safe environment for them by being transparent yourself and engaging their hearts. These women may not care as much about head knowledge and may care more deeply how knowledge about God applies to their lives. They want to avoid being put in a box. Keep the focus on applying truth to their lives and they will stay engaged. Don't preach to them; be real and show them through your experiences how to pursue the mind of Christ.

## PRAGMATIC LEARNERS

These women are more accustomed to a traditional, inductive, or precept approach to Bible study. They have a high value for truth and authority but may not place as high a value on the emotional aspects of confessing sin and being vulnerable. To them it may feel unnecessary or dramatic. Keep the focus on the truth of Scripture. These women keep truth in the forefront of their lives and play a valuable role in discipleship.

Because this study is different from traditional studies, some women may need more time to get used to the approach of this study. The goal is still to make God big in our lives, to fix our minds on Him, and to choose where to train our thoughts. We all just approach it in unique ways to reach unique types of people. I actually wrote this study praying it could reach both types of learners. I am one who lives with a foot in both worlds, trying to apply the deep truths I gained in seminary in an experiential way. I pray that this study would deeply engage the heart and the mind, and that we would be people who worship God in spirit and in truth, not just learning about the battle for our minds but going to war for them together.

# SESSION 1

## INTRODUCTION: ARE YOU TIRED?

Note to Leader: The teaching format for this session is different than the other sessions because it is the first group time and there is no personal study to review.

## 1. OPEN

Welcome the women to your group and take a few moments for introductions. Briefly share about yourself and allow the other women to do the same. After the introductions, lead the group in prayer.

Distribute the Bible study guides to group members and go over the Instructions and Expectations on page 4. Explain and show the women their individual access to Streaming Video so everyone can keep up with the study, regardless of an unavoidable missed gathering.

## 2. WATCH

View the Session 1 video.

## 3. DISCUSS

Provide time for women to read the Introduction lesson to themselves. Take a few minutes to discuss the content. Use the following questions as discussion prompts:

- Do you ever feel like you're living your life to prove something? Explain.

- Review "If I Were Your Enemy." With which part of that section did you most relate? Why?

- Read Jeremiah 2:13. Are you settling for broken cisterns? If so, how?

Direct women to answer the questions on pages 16–18. After they have completed the questions, take a few minutes to discuss their answers.

## 4. ASK

Transition to the Conversation Cards to continue your discussion. The cards for this week are labeled "Introduction" on the front. Lead women to choose, answer, and discuss the questions on the cards. (You can review the instructions for using the cards in "SESSION FORMAT" on page 195.)

## 5. CLOSE

Close by asking women to write down three things:

- one thing they learned from this session;

- one reason they are excited about this study;

- one question they have moving forward.

Briefly discuss their responses. Do so with little or no commentary, but paying close attention to the answers. If time allows, close by praying specifically for each woman in your group, using one of each woman's responses as the focus of your prayer for her.

Encourage women to complete Session 2 Study and Experiences before the next group meeting.

# SESSION 2

## FULFILLED: THE END OF THIRST

*MAIN IDEA: We have substituted the real joy found in Jesus with the world's cheap imitations. We need to drink the new wine Jesus offers to satisfy our thirsty souls.*

This week we will look at the story in John 2 of Jesus turning water to wine. With this first miracle Jesus was pointing to a new kind of life found only in Him. Help the women know that all they are longing for can be found in Christ.

Here are some general goals and thoughts for your time together this week:

- Continue to foster a safe environment for women to share their hearts.

- Help women honestly assess where they are turning for fulfillment.

- Make clear that Jesus is the only One who brings true fulfillment.

- Help them understand what an abundant life in Christ looks like.

*MAIN GOAL: Challenge women to quit trying to be fulfilled in what the world offers and find true joy in Jesus.*

## 1. OPEN

Begin by reviewing the personal study from last week. Here are some suggested places to focus as you review:

- What truths stood out to you from the story of Jesus turning the water to wine in John 2?

- Why do you think this was Jesus' first miracle? What was His purpose?

- What metaphorical cheap wine do you turn to most often instead of turning to Jesus?

- Share what you learned from Experience 4.

- What else stood out to you from the lesson and Scripture that you need to learn, treasure, and/or apply?

## 2. WATCH

Share supplemental teaching and view the video for Session 2 – Fulfilled: The End of Thirst.

## 3. ASK

Transition to the Conversation Cards to continue your discussion. The cards for this week are labeled "Fulfilled" on the front. Lead women to choose, answer, and discuss the questions on the cards. (You can review the instructions for using the cards in "SESSION FORMAT" on page 195.)

## 4. CLOSE

Save for last the Conversation Card that asks, "What is one change you need to make in your life because of what you experienced this week?" Encourage women to choose a partner and share their answers to that question with each other. Then challenge them to pray for each other to have the strength and courage to make that change.

Encourage women to complete Session 3 Study and Experiences before the next group meeting.

# SESSION 3

## CONNECTED: THE END OF LONELINESS

*MAIN IDEA: We all long for connection. But true connection with others only comes after we are in a relationship with Jesus.*

This week we will look at the story in John 4 of Jesus and the Samaritan woman at the well. This woman had a deep longing in her spirit, a desire for true connection. Yet her life was filled with broken relationships and shame. Only after she met Jesus did her life change.

Here are some general goals and thoughts for your time together this week:

- Recognize that many of us are surrounded by people, but filled with loneliness.

- Note how Jesus was fully present with this woman even though culture said He shouldn't be seen with her.

- Challenge women to be fully present in their relationships with Jesus and with others.

*MAIN GOAL: Help women find true connection in a relationship with Jesus.*

## 1. OPEN

Begin by reviewing the personal study from last week. Here are some suggested places to focus as you review:

- How does true connection risk all that we are and cost our whole selves?

- What barriers did Jesus push through to develop a relationship with the woman at the well? What barriers keep you from developing relationships with others?

- In what ways did her life change through her encounter with Jesus and what was the evidence?

- How has Jesus been fully present in His relationship with you?

- Share about the connections you made in Experiences 2 and 3.

- What else stood out to you from the lesson and Scripture that you need to learn, treasure, and/or apply?

## 2. WATCH

Share supplemental teaching and watch the video teaching for Session 3 – Connected: The End of Loneliness.

## 3. ASK

Transition to the Conversation Cards to continue your discussion. The cards for this week are labeled "Connected" on the front. Lead women to choose, answer, and discuss the questions on the cards. (You can review the instructions for using the cards in "SESSION FORMAT" on page 195.)

## 4. CLOSE

Circle your group and hold hands. Encourage them to be closely connected to Jesus and to each other this week. Close with prayer.

Encourage women to complete Session 4 Study and Experiences before the next group meeting.

# SESSION 4

## REST: THE END OF STRIVING

*MAIN IDEA: Our souls are weary and need to find true rest in Jesus.*

We will examine two stories in John 6 and see how Jesus modeled freedom from striving and the joy of dependence.

Here are some general goals and thoughts for your time together this week:

- Define and describe striving and why it is so detrimental to our relationship with Jesus.

- Recognize how we are striving and what it looks like to rest in Christ.

- Realize how much fear plays into our striving and challenge women to remember that no matter what happens to them they are secure in Jesus.

*MAIN GOAL: Lead women to quit relying on their own power and trust the power of God.*

## 1. OPEN

Begin by reviewing the personal study from last week. Here are some suggested places to focus as you review:

- Share a personal experience of striving. Then allow women to share their similar stories.

- How did Jesus challenge Philip in John 6:5–7? Would you have reacted any differently? Explain.

- How does Jesus bring peace into your chaos?

- Share about your time of Sabbath rest from Experience 2 and your plan for rest from Experience 4.

- What else stood out to you from the lesson and Scripture that you need to learn, treasure, and/or apply?

## 2. WATCH

Share supplemental teaching and view the video for Session 4 – Rest: The End of Striving.

## 3. ASK

Transition to the Conversation Cards to continue your discussion. The cards for this week are labeled "Rest" on the front. Lead women to choose, answer, and discuss the questions on the cards. (You can review the instructions for using the cards in "SESSION FORMAT" on page 195.)

## 4. CLOSE

Close by sharing a personal story of how Jesus provided peace and rest for you in the time of a storm. Ask if any group member is going through a time of storms right now. If one or more women indicate this is true in their lives, circle around them and pray for them.

Encourage women to complete Session 5 Study and Experiences before the next group meeting.

# SESSION 5

## RISK: THE END OF PASSIVITY

*MAIN IDEA: Jesus often moves through godly, obedient risk.*

The story of the man born blind in John 9 will show us how Jesus risked to set a man free and how the man risked to gain that freedom.

Here are some general goals and thoughts for your time together this week:

- Discover what it means to risk for God and why it's so necessary.

- Reflect on how many of us are living for something worth dying for.

- Discuss how many of us will go through our Christian lives and risk very little for the cause of Christ.

- Emphasize that risking for Jesus is worth it.

*MAIN GOAL: Challenge women to not settle for comfortable, but be willing to give up everything to follow Jesus.*

## 1. OPEN

Begin by reviewing the personal study from last week. Here are some suggested places to focus as you review:

- What does risking for Jesus mean to you?

- Of all the people in the John 9 story, who do you most associate with and why?

- What is your greatest hindrance in risking for Christ?

- Tell us about your risk adventure from Experience 2.

- What else stood out to you from the lesson and Scripture that you need to learn, treasure, and/or apply?

## 2. WATCH

Share supplemental teaching and view the video for Session 5 – Risk: The End of Passivity.

## 3. ASK

Transition to the Conversation Cards to continue your discussion. The cards for this week are labeled "Risk" on the front. Lead women to choose, answer, and discuss the questions on the cards. (You can review the instructions for using the cards in "SESSION FORMAT" on page 195.)

## 4. CLOSE

Challenge each member of your group to pray a prayer of total surrender such as, "Lord, I'll do anything you want me to do." Encourage them to write the prayer in their book or Bible and date it. Emphasize that this is not a prayer to pray flippantly or take lightly. Provide a quiet moment for them to consider this challenge, then close with prayer.

Encourage women to complete Session 6 Study and Experiences before the next group meeting.

# SESSION 6

## HOPE: THE END OF FEAR

*MAIN IDEA: Suffering here on earth is unavoidable. But even in the darkest times, perhaps especially in the darkest times, we find hope in the power and presence of Christ.*

In John 11, Jesus intentionally waits to visit a sick and dying friend. He was not being cruel, but used this moment to display His authority over His greatest enemy and show that real hope is found in Him.

Here are some general goals and thoughts for your time together this week:

- Discuss how we spend a lot of time figuring out how we can avoid suffering.

- Emphasize that though we try to avoid suffering, life is filled with difficult times and all of us are going to walk through them.

- Embrace the truth that sometimes God uses suffering to grow our faith.

- Make sure we are putting our hope in the right thing, the right Person.

*MAIN GOAL: Help women see that God wants to use our suffering and dark times to grow us and glorify Himself.*

## 1. OPEN

Begin by reviewing the personal study from last week. Here are some suggested places to focus as you review:

- We say we believe that God is sovereign and that everything Jesus does and says and allows to transpire is for our good and His glory, but do we really believe that? Explain.

- Put yourself in Mary's and Martha's shoes. How would you have responded to Jesus? Have you cried out to Him in a similar way over a current or past situation? Explain.

- Share your responses from Experience 1.

- What else stood out to you from the lesson and Scripture that you need to learn, treasure, and/or apply?

## 2. WATCH

Share supplemental teaching and view the video for Session 6 – Hope: The End of Fear.

## 3. ASK

Transition to the Conversation Cards to continue your discussion. The cards for this week are labeled "Hope" on the front. Lead women to choose, answer, and discuss the questions on the cards. (You can review the instructions for using the cards in "SESSION FORMAT" on page 195.)

## 4. CLOSE

Share a personal experience of how Jesus carried you through a time of suffering. Allow the women to share similar stories. If a member of your group is currently walking through a dark time, take a moment to surround her and pray for her.

Encourage women to complete Session 7 Study and Experiences before the next group meeting.

# SESSION 7

## GRACE: THE END OF SHAME

*MAIN IDEA: As we are honest about our sin, we experience the cleansing of Christ's forgiveness.*

The story of Jesus washing His disciples' feet in John 13 is filled with humiliation. From Jesus humbling Himself to this servant task to the disciples allowing their feet to be washed, we feel the call to be cleansed to serve.

Here are some general goals and thoughts for your time together this week:

- Discuss how exposing our sin is not something most of us long to do.

- Emphasize that only those who receive cleansing from Jesus will become a part of Him.

- Point out that it's spiritually healthy for us to share our struggle with sin with each other.

- State that we can't move forward in freedom as long as we are in bondage to our sin.

*MAIN GOAL: Challenge the women to be honest about their sin, allow Jesus to cleanse them, and walk in the freedom of His grace.*

## 1. OPEN

Begin by reviewing the personal study from last week. Here are some suggested places to focus as you review:

- How is being caught a great gift?

- Why was Peter unsettled by Jesus wanting to wash His feet? What lesson was Jesus teaching?

- What causes us to struggle with confessing our sins?

- Share your responses from Experiences 3 and 4 about experiencing grace from Christ and expressing that grace to someone else.

- What else stood out to you from the lesson and Scripture that you need to learn, treasure, and/or apply?

## 2. WATCH

Share supplemental teaching and view the video for Session 7 – Grace: The End of Shame.

## 3. ASK

Transition to the Conversation Cards to continue your discussion. The cards for this week are labeled "Grace" on the front. Lead women to choose, answer, and discuss the questions on the cards. (You can review the instructions for using the cards in "SESSION FORMAT" on page 195.)

## 4. CLOSE

Talk about how our struggle with sin is so raw and real. Emphasize again that everyone in the group is in the same boat, sinners set free from sin but still struggling to walk in holiness. Cheer your group on, encouraging them to be honest about their sin before the Lord. Invite several women to pray to close your time together.

Encourage women to complete Session 8 Study and Experiences before the next group meeting.

# SESSION 8

## CALLED: THE END OF EMPTINESS

*MAIN IDEA: We tend to make our relationships with God about doing for Him, which is definitely a part. However, it's most important that we first be with Him.*

In John 21 we see some of the disciples endure a fruitless night of fishing. After a command from shore results in a net full of fish, they realize the issuer of the command is the risen Lord. Peter swims to shore, while the others follow in the boat. When they get to shore, they sit around the fire and enjoy breakfast with Jesus.

Here are some general goals and thoughts for your time together this week:

- Understand that being with Jesus comes before doing for Jesus.

- Realize that many of the expectations placed on our Christian lives are ours, not God's.

- Be reminded that God is not asking us to prove something to Him, but to love and enjoy Him.

*MAIN GOAL: Help women understand and embrace the true mission: love God and love others.*

## 1. OPEN

Begin by reviewing the personal study from last week. Here are some suggested places to focus as you review:

- What if we all just did what God put into us to do every day?

- In John 21, what was significant about Jesus having breakfast with His men?

- Do you take time to have breakfast with Jesus? Explain.

- Share your mission statements that you created in Experience 3. What was challenging about that exercise? What was freeing?

- What else stood out to you from the lesson and Scripture that you need to learn, treasure, and/or apply?

## 2. WATCH

Share supplemental teaching and view the video for Session 8 – Called: The End of Emptiness.

## 3. ASK

Transition to the Conversation Cards to continue your discussion. The cards for this week are labeled "Called" on the front. Lead women to choose, answer, and discuss the questions on the cards. (You can review the instructions for using the cards in "SESSION FORMAT" on page 195.)

## 4. CLOSE

Lead your group to read the commission (page 185) silently. Briefly discuss which statements speak most deeply to them. Then read it aloud together. Close with a prayer time of surrender and commitment.

# SCRIPTURE USED IN VIDEO SESSIONS

## SESSION 1 - Introduction

Matthew 11:28–30
Romans 3:23
John 7:37–38
Isaiah 12:3
Jeremiah 2:13
2 Corinthians 3:4–5

## SESSION 2 - Fulfilled

John 2:1–12
Matthew 26:26–30
Psalm 4:7
Joel 2:19

## SESSION 3 - Connected

John 4

## SESSION 4 - Rest

John 6:1–13
Psalm 46:10

## SESSION 5 - Risk

John 9
Hebrews 11:1

## SESSION 6 - Hope

John 11

## SESSION 7 - Grace

John 13:1–20
Proverbs 11:2
1 John 1:5–7,10
John 21:15
1 Peter 2:24–25

## SESSION 8 - Called

John 21
Matthew 10:39

# ENDNOTES

1. joy, *Dictionary.com Unabridged*, Random House, Inc., http://www.dictionary.com/browse/joy

2. entertainment, *Dictionary.com Unabridged*, Random House, Inc., http://www.dictionary.com/browse/entertainment

3. John Owen, *The Mortification of Sin* (Trinity Press, 2013), 9.

4. Mandy Len Catron, "To Fall in Love With Anyone, Do This," *The New York Times*, January 9, 2015, http://www.nytimes.com/2015/01/11/fashion/modern-love-to-fall-in-love-with-anyone-do-this.html

5. Bob Deffinbaugh, "The Light of the World (John 9:1-41)," *bible.org*, June 1, 2004. https://bible.org/seriespage/12-light-world-john-91-41

6. Arthur Bennett, ed., *The Valley of Vision* (Edinburgh, United Kingdom: Banner of Truth Trust, 1975), 75.

# ABOUT THE AUTHOR

Jennie Allen is an author, speaker, and the founder and visionary of IF:Gathering. She is a passionate leader following God's call on her life to catalyze a generation to live what they believe. Jennie is the author of *Made for This*, *Anything*, *Nothing to Prove*, and her most recent *New York Times* bestselling book, *Get Out of Your Head*. Her Bible studies include *Stuck*, *Chase*, *Restless*, and *Get Out of Your Head*. Jennie has a master's in biblical studies from Dallas Theological Seminary and lives in Dallas, Texas, with her husband, Zac, and their four children.

# NO MORE PRETENDING.
# NO MORE PERFORMING.
# NO MORE FIGHTING
# TO PROVE YOURSELF.

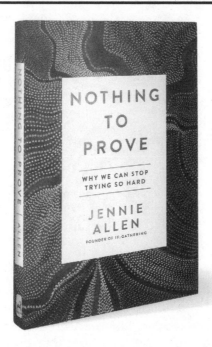

Jesus didn't save you so you could try harder. So you could fear more. So you could struggle to be enough. He came that you might have life and have it abundantly. In *Nothing to Prove*, Jennie Allen offers us the freedom to rest in the grace of God's enough-ness.

WATERBROOK

# Also Available from
# *jennie allen*

## Stopping The Spiral of Toxic Thoughts

In *Get Out of Your Head*, a six-session, video-based Bible study, Jennie inspires and equips us to transform our emotions, our outlook, and even our circumstances by taking control of our thoughts. Our enemy is determined to get in our heads to make us feel helpless, overwhelmed, and incapable of making a difference for the kingdom of God. But when we submit our minds to Christ, the promises and goodness of God flood our lives in remarkable ways.

Visit **JennieAllen.com** for more info about *Get Out of Your Head*.

Available wherever books & Bibles are sold.

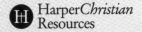

# Also Available from
# jennie allen

## Identify the threads of your life

In this DVD-based study using the story of Joseph, Jennie explains how his suffering, gifts, story, and relationships fit into the greater story of God— and how your story can do the same. She introduces Threads—a tool to help you see your own personal story and to uncover and understand the raw materials God has given you to use for his glory and purpose.

Visit **JennieAllen.com** for more info about *Restless*.

Available wherever books & Bibles are sold.

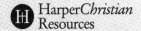

# Also Available from
# jennie allen

## Chasing After the Heart of God

*Chase* is a Bible study experience to discover the heart of God and what it is exactly He wants from us. As we work through major events in the life of David, and the Psalms he wrote out of those experiences, you see a man who was reckless and imperfect but possessed the favor of God. Whether you are running from God or working your tail off to please Him, this man's journey will challenge your view of God.

Visit **JennieAllen.com** for more info about *Chase*.

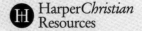

# Also Available from
## jennie allen

## The Places We Get Stuck & the God Who Sets Us Free

Women are hurting. A lot of us feel stuck. This is not a novel perception—this is human. We are stuck trying to be perfect. Stuck in sadness. Stuck feeling numb. Stuck pursuing more stuff to make us happy. Stuck in something we can't even name. *Stuck* is an eight-session Bible study experience leading women to the invisible struggles that we fight and to the God who has to set us free.

Visit **JennieAllen.com** for more info about *Stuck*.

Available wherever books & Bibles are sold.

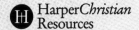